A Fresh Tart in a Small Town
Recipes from La Musette in Niwot

This cookbook is dedicated to Dakota. I hope your story is also a winding tale of adventures with many chapters, a loving community, and delectable morsels.

A Fresh Tart in a Small Town
Recipes from La Musette in Niwot

Written by Skyla V. Olds
Designed & Illustrated by SJ Gingras

Acknowledgements

I feel overwhelming gratitude to everyone who supported La Musette and encouraged me to create this cookbook.

To SJ Gingras, my amazing graphic designer and wonderful partner in this endeavor, I love how you wrangled my chaotic and demanding ideas into such a beautiful work. You were an unexpected pleasure in this process.

To Paloma and Dakota, thank you for joining me at La Musette, for flying in from California to work in the food truck when needed (and, in Dakota's case, for an entire summer) and for being an effervescent part of my Niwot chapter.

To all who worked at the Wheel House and La Musette during my tenure there, I appreciate the hard work, the support, and vibrant company. The small moments of working together, eating together, kvetching together and bickering together filled my days during three good years of life. Thank you Eric for bringing us all together.

To the Niwot community, thank you for welcoming me to this town, supporting my endeavors, becoming my friends, following my culinary excursions and helping to anchor my new life.

To Maggie, my extraordinary friend and editor, you are and have always been a shining and guiding star in my universe. It is simultaneously unbelievable and so right that we worked on this book together, some thirty-five years after "borrowing" office supplies as the student office aides in elementary school. Your opinion has always been of the utmost value to me and your words after reviewing some very rough drafts buoyed me to the finish line. To Diane Winters and others who read sections, thank you for the final round of careful proofreading.

To my family, I am fortunate to have been so loved in my life. That love has enabled me to go out into the world and pursue new endeavors, ones for which I was arguably under-prepared and possibly under-qualified, with the confidence that it will all turn out okay, somehow. I have learned so much about cooking and life from all of you.

To Zabrina, Nic, Abby, and Naomi, you pushed me to turn my rough La Musette notebook into an actual cookbook. Without your enthusiasm, recipe testing, unwavering faith in my abilities, and early beta reading of the first chapters, this project would have remained an aspirational book in my head.

To the Pooks, thank you for the love, advice and support. To Melanie, Cyril, Liam and Noelle, who brought me to Colorado, provided me with a sense of family and home here, and were among the most critical taste-tasters, thank you.

To the Sky crew, the many many people over several decades who have helped out at Sky, who have shared in the making and consuming of great wines and food, celebrated with us during the good times and shared our grief during the darker days, thank you.

La Musette at THE WHEEL HOUSE

NIWO

TABLE OF

ONTENTS

INTRODUCTION:
LA MUSETTE'S ORIGIN STORY

La Musette's Origin Story

2017 was a fiery inferno. I was living in the Sonoma Valley running my family's small vineyard and winery, Sky Vineyards, while practicing criminal defense law. It was a strange harvest where extreme weather patterns had increasingly become the norm. On October 8, 2017, I spent the day helping friends crush grapes at their winery and then headed up the hill, to the top of Mt. Veeder, for a family dinner. Unbeknownst to all of us, this was to be a Last Supper of sorts. My sisters, my niece, my father, his partner, and a few friends gathered around our kitchen table—the table my father made by hand in his youth—for a rambunctious, joyful, and delicious dinner. There was laughter, wine, and an amazing harvest meal as we gathered in the candle-lit coziness of the rustic home I was born and raised in. Outside, a ferocious hot wind battered the trees, causing my 8-year-old niece Dakota to remark "this wind feels dangerous." Indeed.

Memories of the dinner are seared into my brain, some moments so vivid that it felt like last night, with other moments hazy and half-forgotten as if from a movie I saw decades ago. It would have been a normal harvest meal at Sky, much like hundreds of others I have enjoyed throughout my life—full of friends and family, laughter, bickering, zinfandel and always the most flavorful and soul-satisfying food—but for the catastrophic events that followed.

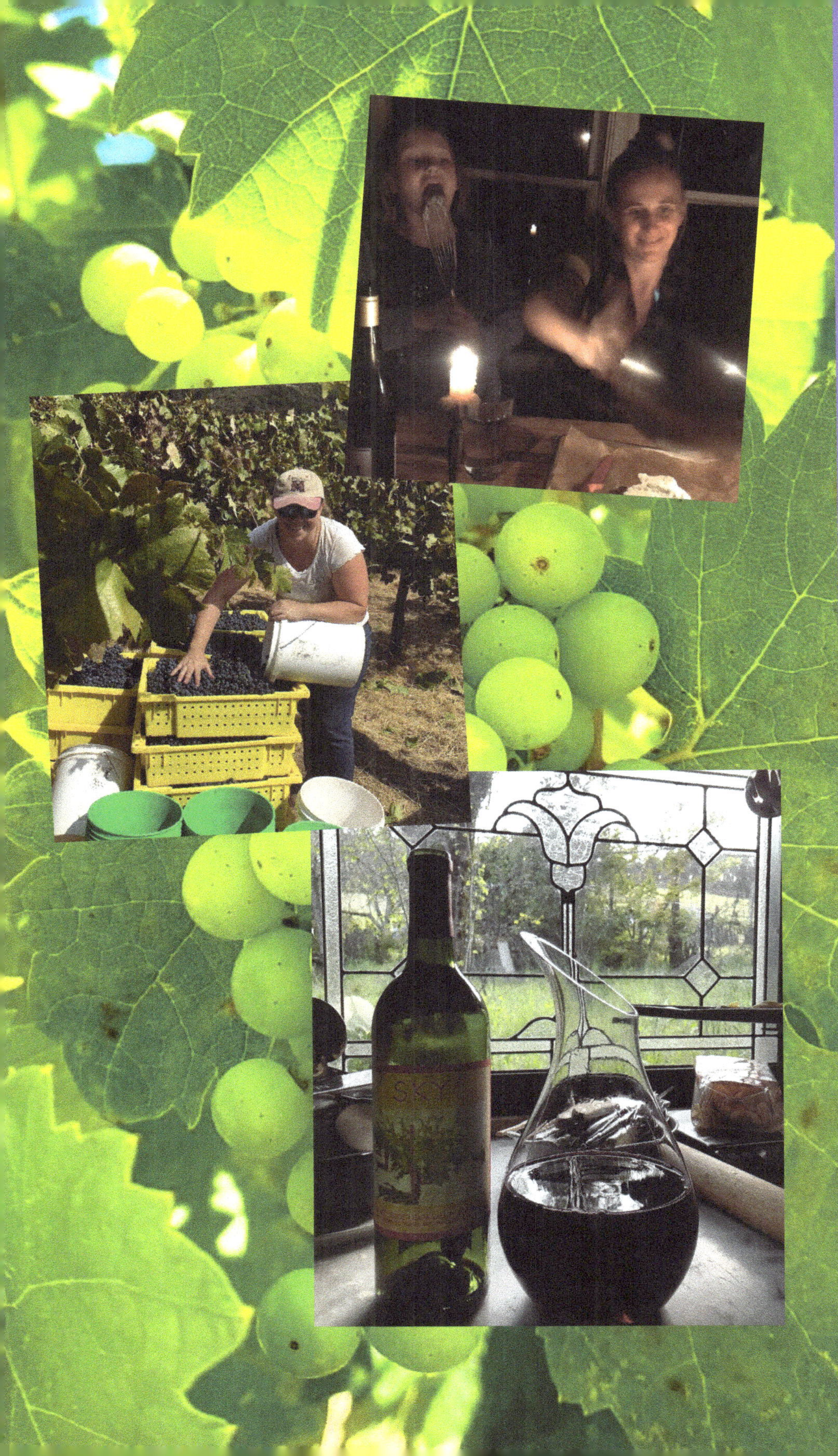

Over the next ten days, my family, friends, neighbors and I lived in a smokey hellscape as the various wildfires—later referred to as the North Bay Fire Complex—raged through Sonoma and Napa Valleys. We left our homes in the middle of the night, watched encroaching flames, slept on floors, checked in on relatives and the firefighters we knew (including my uncle and two cousins), and lived in a hazy apocalyptic reality. By the end of those days, my cottage, my niece's home, and the two childhood homes I grew up in that were the current residences for my father and cousin, had all burned to the ground.

The vineyard, the home my family had built by hand (and site of that Last Supper) and 99% of my family's property on the top of Mt. Veeder were torched as three raging wildfires converged at Sky. The physical and emotional devastation to me, my family, and our community are difficult to describe. I spent the next year trying to rebuild some semblance of a life for us—overseeing the Kafkaesque process of EPA cleanup, insurance claims, wildfire litigation, obtaining temporary housing for myself and my father, navigating a possible rebuild and cobbling the family business back together.

By October 2018, after setting Sky on the recovery path, I realized I needed to leave California and try to get my own life back on track. I had experienced severe PTSD from the fires and essentially lost a year of my life trying to recover and rebuild the family home and winery. I felt like an empty shell. Over the next few years, I wandered the world, trying to find a home, a relationship, or a job to anchor me back to my own existence. I traveled, lived with friends, started cooking professionally and eventually, unexpectedly, fortuitously, found myself in Colorado.

8

In May 2021, I met with Eric Bergeson at the Wheel House in Niwot, Colorado. At the time, the Wheel House was a community hub with a bar, a stage for live music and events, seating for 70 people, and a bike shop. Eric had just obtained a food trailer and was looking for someone to run the food truck as a kitchen for the community bar. One of my secret dreams had been to take over a small diner in the middle of nowhere and start feeding an unsuspecting community the foods I loved throughout my life. Faced with the golden opportunity of my secret fantasy served up on a silver platter, I had no choice but to move to Niwot and open La Musette.

And so La Musette was born. For the next three and half years, I cooked whatever I wanted and shared the foods I had grown up with and discovered throughout my travels with the Niwot community. I changed the menu weekly, followed the seasons, and integrated the vibrant Niwot community events into my menus.

My approach to cooking is intimate and personal. I make dishes that share who I am, where I have been and what I believe. The act of sharing through food creates connection and relationship. The folks that welcomed and supported me over those years were not merely "customers," but became my friends and my community. Through La Musette, I was finally able to find the anchors to rebuild my own life and recover from the trauma of the 2017 fires.

I closed La Musette in December 2024. This cookbook is intended as way to continue to feed and nourish the Niwot community, to whom I owe so much; a way to memorialize the special time in Niwot that I feel so fortunate to have been a part of; and a way to continue sharing my love of good food. These are some of the recipes that I developed or used over the past several years at La Musette. I hope they become a part of your lives and in some small way help to promote the connection and community that we all need as we strive for meaning in our lives, as they have helped in mine.

NIWOT'S HONEYBEE FESTIVAL

Grandma Olds's coriander
honey spice bread

Beef chili with fennel
pollen crema

Mayacamas's cornbread
with honey butter

Fried squash blossoms stuffed
with herbed goat cheese

Toasty bread with ricotta,
grilled peaches, drizzled
honey and hazelnuts

Prosciutto and melon with
honey-mint drizzle

CHAPTER 1
Niwot's HoneyBee Festival

Niwot is undoubtedly the Stars Hollow of Colorado. The small unincorporated community is led by the local business association (the "NBA") and hosts monthly events that bring folks out, dressing up and reveling in the closed down streets of the historic district. From the windows of La Musette, situated between the post office and the Wheel House on Murray street, I saw Santa Claus on a horse drawn carriage, regulars driving tractors and classic cars, dogs dressed as honeybees, adults lit up with LED suits, and kids untethered, happy and running to the park. With parades, summer concert series, dancing under the stars, flower festivals, Oktoberfests, and Halloween pet costume contests, Niwot community events provide the excuse folks need to come together, carouse, and support the locals.

Among my favorite events was the annual HoneyBee Festival, held every fall. My first HoneyBee festival came a week after I opened and almost did me in. It was my first chance to see how Niwot loves to come out and party in the streets. Every year for my HoneyBee Festival menu I went through several quarts of Niwot beekeepers Dawn and Jeff Server's vibrant Meadow Lake Honey.

It was during successive HoneyBee festivals that I realized La Musette was officially a part of the Niwot community: folks began anticipating my grandmother's coriander spiced honey bread weeks before the HoneyBee festival rolled around.

The term "la musette" in French means "the bag" and refers to a small lunch sack that you hand to bicyclists during races to eat while riding. Eric came up with the name to connect the food trailer to the bike theme of the Niwot Wheel Works shop and Wheel House bar.

Grandma Olds's coriander honey spice bread

This honey bread is one of the most beloved of my family recipes. The aroma of warm coriander and honey baking transports me to my grandmother's kitchen and is one of the distinctive smells of holidays and harvest. Grandma Olds originally found this recipe in Gene Opton's 1979 Honey Feast cookbook and baked it for harvest lunches at the vineyard, slicing it up with cold pork roast and homemade mayo for the best sandwich you've never had. Ethiopian in origin, the bread is both savory and a touch sweet, with beautiful texture and a heady aroma. After showcasing it during the first HoneyBee festival, several La Musette regulars eagerly awaited its return and would make sure to swing by early during the festival, lest I ran out.

INGREDIENTS

2 Tbsp dry yeast

2 tsp sugar

¼ tsp ground ginger

2 eggs

1 cup local honey

2 Tbsp roughly ground coriander seeds (I use a mortar and pestle)

1 tsp ground cinnamon

½ tsp ground cloves

1 Tbsp salt

9 cups flour

Mix together in a large bowl the dry yeast, ½ cup warm water, the sugar and the ginger. Let sit for 10 minutes as you work on the next steps.

Meanwhile, using a stand mixer with a paddle attachment, mix eggs, honey, coriander seeds, cinnamon, cloves and salt. In a small saucepan or in a microwave, heat but do not boil the milk and butter. Wait until cool enough to comfortably touch, and then add to the egg and honey mixture, stirring on low to incorporate. Add 2 cups of flour and mix on low until fully incorporated. Then add the bubbling yeast mixture. After mixing that in, add 7 more cups of flour and mix again on low.

The dough should come together. Do not knead or overmix. Cover with a clean linen towel or plastic wrap and let rise for 2 hours or until doubled in size.

Punch the dough down, divide into two rounds and place in a buttered soufflé dish or other deep baking dish. I have also shaped into 8 smaller buns at this point or placed two large loaves free standing on a baking sheet. Allow to rise another hour, covered.

Bake loaves for 50-60 minutes at 300°F and smaller buns for 30 minutes. After removing the bread from the oven, allow it to rest for 5 minutes. If it is in a baking dish, loosen the edges with a knife and dump the bread out of the dish. Let cool fully on a wire rack.

 In addition to slicing for sandwiches, the honey bread is heavenly when toasted and buttered or smothered with cream cheese.

Beef chili with fennel pollen crema

Since the HoneyBee festival was really a celebration of all pollinators, thematic foods for the menu encompassed flowers and pollen in addition to honey. The "dress your pet as your favorite pollinator" costumes included dogs dressed as bats and hummingbirds, as well as bees.

To fortify Niwotians for the day of activities and fun, I offered a hearty beef chili garnished with sour cream and fennel pollen. Fennel pollen can be sourced from your garden, local farms, gourmet specialty stores or online. I have bronze fennel volunteering in my garden so I collect the pollen, leaving half of the fronds to turn to seed for a later harvesting of fennel seeds. A small pinch of pollen goes a long way, which is good since a small pinch of pollen is all you will likely get from a couple plants!

INGREDIENTS

1 pound Rancho Gordo dried cranberry beans, soaked overnight

1½ pounds ground beef or cubed steak

1 onion, diced

½ fennel bulb, diced

2 cloves garlic, minced

1 Tbsp ground cumin

1 tsp smoked paprika

1-2 tsp Burlap & Barrel Kashmiri chili powder

1 large tomato, diced

1 poblano chili, fire-roasted, peeled and diced
(see page 159)

1 quart chicken or beef stock, preferably homemade

1 bay leaf

Salt

Pepper

If you don't have chicken or beef stock, you can use the bean cooking liquid for your chili liquid later.

GARNISH

Sour cream

Fennel pollen

Cheddar cheese

Scallions, chopped

Cilantro, chopped

Cook soaked dried beans in their soaking water with 2 teaspoons salt and a bay leaf for 30 minutes or until soft. If you don't have chicken or beef stock, you can use the bean cooking liquid for your chili liquid later.

In a large pot on medium high heat, pour enough olive oil to coat the bottom. Sauté the chopped onion with a pinch of salt until softened. Then add the chopped fennel and continue sautéing, stirring often. Add more olive oil if the pot looks dry or the vegetables start to darken. After a few minutes, add the ground beef and continue to stir regularly. Salt and pepper the meat generously (about 2 teaspoons of salt and ½ teaspoon black pepper). After a few minutes, add the minced garlic, cumin, paprika and chili powder. Stir for another minute. Add the diced tomato and sauté for another minute. Finally, add the diced poblano, the cooked beans and either the stock or the bean water.

Lower to a simmer and cook for at least 40 minutes and up to 2 hours, with the lid slightly askew. Stir periodically and add more liquid if needed.

After the first half hour, taste the chili and add more salt, pepper and/or spices to your taste. If the chili is too liquidy, remove the lid and let it evaporate some to thicken while cooking.

Serve with your choice of any or all of the garnish, ending with a dollop of sour cream and a sprinkle of fennel pollen.

Mayacamas's cornbread with honey butter

My older sister Mayacamas has many dietary restrictions and feeding her is one of the reasons I always tried at La Musette to offer substitutions and accommodations. I understand how difficult it can be to eat in restaurants when there are specific ingredients you need to avoid and I wanted La Musette to be as friendly as possible to customers like my sister. Mayacamas's awesome cornbread recipe, which uses a mix of masa harina and fine cornmeal instead of wheat flour, as well as a lot of fresh ingredients, became the basis of my go-to cornbread recipe.

(Although I often added butter, dairy and scallions, all things she cannot eat! Little sisters are brats!)

CORNBREAD

1 cup masa harina

1 cup fine cornmeal

2 Tbsp sugar

2 tsp baking powder

2 tsp baking soda

1 tsp salt

1½ cup buttermilk

⅔ cup melted butter

2 eggs, beaten

4 ears of corn, kernels
cut off cob

1 jalapeño, minced

¼ cup scallion greens,
thinly sliced

HONEY BUTTER

1 stick butter, softened

⅛ cup local honey

½ tsp Maldon salt

Unless a recipe specifies Maldon salt, I use Diamond Crystal brand kosher salt for everything. The salinity of salt varies considerably by brand, so adjust accordingly if using a different brand.

Mix all the dry ingredients together. Add the buttermilk and melted butter and stir until incorporated. Add the eggs and stir until incorporated. Add the fresh corn, jalapeño and scallions and fold into the batter. Pour into a 9 x 9 glass baking dish.

Bake at 375-400ºF for 15-20 minutes.

For the honey butter, mix all the ingredients together with a rubber spatula until uniform. Honey butter will last for several weeks in the fridge.

Serve warm with honey butter.

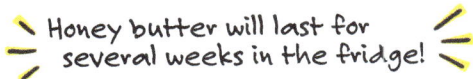

Honey butter will last for several weeks in the fridge!

Fried squash blossoms stuffed with herbed goat cheese

Fried squash blossoms are a holy grail of summer treats. They check many boxes: a vegetarian appetizer that is more delicious even than anything wrapped in bacon; quick and easy to make; elevated and sophisticated to serve; and if you have a summer garden, a better use of your prolific zucchini plant than most recipes!

If you have said garden, pick the orange squash blossoms in the morning while they are still closed. Zucchini and other summer squash plants have both male and female blossoms, but the male blossoms never develop fruit so they are the ones to snip. They are usually further from the center of the plant and lack the bulbous base that will later develop into squash. Keep refrigerated or in water like flowers until ready to use. Blossoms can also be sourced from farmers markets.

Unlike a more traditional Italian deep fried squash blossom, these are very lightly battered and cooked like a pancake in a little oil until golden. The result is light and summery, with crispy edges and a gooey herb-forward center. Whenever these appeared on the La Musette menu, they would fly out of the truck like hotcakes!

INGREDIENTS

12 squash blossoms

4 oz fresh chèvre
(soft fresh goat cheese)

1 large shallot, minced

1 Tbsp butter

2 Tbsp chiffonaded fresh
herbs: chives, basil, thyme,
cilantro, tarragon, in any
combination

½ cup flour

¼ cup milk or water

Salt

Grapeseed oil for cooking

Sauté the minced shallot in butter over medium heat with a pinch of salt until softened, stirring often for about 3-4 minutes. Let cool. Mix the cooled shallots, chèvre, and fresh herbs together in a small bowl with a small rubber spatula until fully incorporated.

Gently open a squash blossom, ensure it is free of bugs, and then insert a generous spoonful-sized dab of the herbed chèvre on a butter knife inside the base of the flower. You can gently use the inside petals to coax and scrape the cheese off the knife if needed. Put the stuffed blossoms in the fridge to firm up while you prepare the batter.

In a large stainless bowl, whisk the flour, milk or water, and a pinch of salt. The runniness of the batter will dictate how thick the coating is. Adjust flour or liquid if desired.

If you prefer gluten free, use the whipped egg technique of the chili rellenos on page 121 instead of this batter.

Heat a cast iron pan to medium and coat with a thin layer of grapeseed oil. Holding the blossoms by the stem, dip the blossom into the pancake batter and allow the excess batter to drip back into the bowl before laying in the hot oil. Do not crowd the pan, but you can cook 4-6 at a time, depending on

the size of your cast iron. Cook for about 3 minutes until golden, using a spatula to peek underneath, then flip, holding the stem with your fingers and a spatula under the blossom. Once the second side has golden brown ridges like a pancake, transfer to a paper towel lined plate. If the blossom is particularly large, you may need to cook it on three sides instead of two.

Serve with a sprinkle of Maldon salt.

Toasty bread with ricotta, grilled peaches, drizzled honey and hazelnuts

Tomato toast, avocado toast, crostini, bruschetta. Put anything on some nice crusty bread and sign me up! Although I usually plan brunch items to appeal either to the sweet or the savory palates, this toast is one of the delightful hybrids that marries the two.

Grilling the peaches intensifies their flavor and their sweetness. It is of course best to use perfectly ripened farmers market peaches at the height of their season, but the beauty of the grilling is that it will coax the best out of even a mediocre peach. So if you are disappointed by some peaches on your counter, toss them with olive oil and Maldon salt and grill them up. In addition to the toast below, grilled peaches pair beautifully with ice cream or as an addition to a green or grain salad.

I have served this toast on Grandma's honey bread, which elevates it with the coriander and peach combination, but it also works well on challah, sourdough, or brioche.

INGREDIENTS

Thick sliced bread

Fresh ricotta, preferably
Bellwether brand

Palisade or other
local peaches

Olive oil

Raw hazelnuts

Maldon salt

Aleppo pepper

To grill the peaches, cut them in half and remove the pit. If your peaches are clings rather than freestone and do not easily come off of the pit, you can cut small sections off the pit. You will end up with about 12 slices rather than halves and they will require more attention to ensure they don't burn. Once pitted, drizzle with a glug of good olive oil and gently toss to coat. Sprinkle with maldon salt.

Grill on fairly high heat until slightly blistered on both sides. If grilling the peach halves, it may take a minute or two per side. If you have already sliced the peaches, check after 30 seconds and be sure they don't fall between the slats. If you do not have a grill available, you can lay the peaches on a baking sheet and broil them. Check frequently when broiling to prevent burning. The peaches should be slightly blistered with golden brown or black spots but not charred. Let cool, then slice if peaches are still halved.

Toast hazelnuts in a 350°F oven for 5-8 minutes, checking for slight browning and removing before they burn. Let cool, then coarsely chop.

Toast the bread. Slather on a layer of ricotta. Cover generously with grilled peaches. Strew the hazelnuts. Drizzle with additional olive oil, and finish with Maldon salt and a pinch of Aleppo pepper.

Prosciutto and melon with honey-mint drizzle

As with any simple dish, the success of this recipe depends entirely upon the quality of ingredients. Late summer in Niwot brings a bounty of perfectly ripe local produce, including Kilt Farms' sublime Tuscan melons. Similar to cantaloupe, these melons are slightly perfumey with a silky orange texture. In selecting a ripe melon (other than watermelon), I always go by smell. If you can't detect a faint but intoxicating aroma by sniffing the base where the melon was attached to the plant, don't buy it.

Prosciutto is always best when freshly sliced from a deli counter into almost translucent paper-thin sheets, but there are some decent prepackaged brands that will do in a pinch. Prosciutto di Parma is the gold standard, but the thinness of the slices is almost more important.

INGREDIENTS

1 perfectly ripe orange-fleshed melon (Tuscan, ambrosia, cantaloupe)

6-12 slices of prosciutto

1-2 sprigs fresh mint

1 tsp local honey

2 Tbsp good olive oil

Maldon salt

Detach the mint leaves from the stems and pound in a mortar and pestle with a tiny pinch of salt. Add the honey and olive oil to the mint paste and stir together.

Cut the melon in half latitudinally and scoop out the seeds. Cut each half into six long slices and cut off the skin. Sprinkle a little Maldon onto the melon slices.

Drape ½-1 piece of prosciutto onto each slice of melon and arrange on a serving platter. Drizzle the mint-honey mixture over the 12 slices of melon and prosciutto and serve.

WEEKEND BRUNCH IN NIWOT

Pancakes with caramel sauce and cardamom butter

Flannel vegetable hash with poached eggs

Cubano with melted fontina, roasted pork and sliced pickle

Challah French toast with strawberries, rhubarb and cream

Crêpes

Apple fritters with powdered sugar

Eggs and chard baked in cream

CHAPTER 2:
Weekend brunch in Niwot

Meeting up with friends for a weekend brunch is one of life's great pleasures. A well-crafted brunch menu offers something sweet, a savory egg dish, something meaty, and something light and lunchy. No matter what you are in the mood for, you should be able to find it on a small brunch menu.

I wanted regular brunch to become a thing at the Wheel House but we could never quite make it work. The Niwot downtown area was quiet on the weekends unless there was a town-wide event. We built enough of a brunch following to have some busy weekends with folks lounging with mimosa and Bloody Marys, but just as often, the weekends would find Michael, the brunch bartender, and me twiddling our thumbs. So La Musette brunch became a special occasion event, popping up for Mother's Day, Easter and other Niwot days.

Pancakes with caramel sauce and cardamom butter

This was a staple for the first year of regular La Musette brunches and was requested for months after the brunch service ended. For the fluffy buttermilk pancakes, I consulted an old edition of the Joy of Cooking. This is my family's go-to reference cookbook, but be sure to find an edition published before the 1980s, preferably from the 50s or 60s. Once they removed the squirrel stew recipes, they also started tweaking some of the old standbys, much to our detriment.

Caramel sauce can be tricky to make at home. You can buy it and save yourself some heartache, but homemade is always better. Making caramel was my Achilles' heel, so I put it on the regular brunch menu to force myself to conquer it. After many failed attempts and discarded recipes (burnt sugar, a broken emulsion, chunky sugar that wouldn't melt), this recipe emerged as fairly foolproof. Make a large batch and use it on everything (ice cream, lattes, poached pears, pies).

The cardamom butter was inspired by my love of my grandmother's orange rolls and Nilofer Ichaporia King's cardamom tea cake. Both the butter and caramel sauce will last in the fridge for at least a month.

PANCAKES

1 cup flour

½ tsp salt

1 tsp sugar

¾ tsp baking powder

½ tsp baking soda

1 egg

1 cup buttermilk

2 Tbsp melted butter

Combine the first five dry ingredients in a large mixing bowl. Stir together the egg and buttermilk and then add to dry ingredients, mixing briefly to incorporate. Add the melted butter and stir only as much as necessary. For thinner pancakes, add an extra tablespoon of buttermilk or water.

Heat a griddle or cast iron pan to medium heat. Add a small pat of butter and ladle three pancakes worth of batter into the pan. Flip after about 2 minutes, once small bubbles appear on the top of the pancakes and peeking underneath reveals a golden brown bottom. Add more butter as you flip the pancakes and cook the other side until golden brown. Continue making three pancakes at a time until the batter is used up.

Serve hot with the caramel sauce and cardamom orange butter found on the next pages.

Pancakes with caramel sauce and cardamom butter

CARAMEL SAUCE

2 cups sugar

12 Tbsp butter, cut into 1 Tbsp cubes

1 cup heavy cream

1 tsp Maldon salt

Melt the sugar in a heavy-bottomed pan over medium low heat, stirring often with a heatproof rubber spatula. This will take a few minutes. If the sugar is not turning to liquid, slowly turn the heat up but be careful not to burn the sugar.

Once the sugar has turned to liquid, switch to a wire whisk and begin adding the butter, one tablespoon at a time, whisking well in between additions. After adding all the butter, slowly pour in the cream while continuing to whisk vigorously. Once the cream is fully incorporated and the caramel is smooth, remove the pan from heat and add the salt. Transfer to a glass mason jar and clean the pan and whisk immediately (it will be a nightmare if you let it harden).

The caramel can be kept in the fridge. To use, warm in the microwave or a water bath until the caramel is soft enough to drizzle.

ORANGE CARDAMOM BUTTER

1 stick butter, softened

1 navel orange, washed well

1 tsp cardamom seeds

Maldon salt

Be sure to use cardamom seeds rather than cardamom pods. There are a couple seeds in each pod but rather than opening the fibrous pods yourself, it's easier to buy a jar of just seeds.

Place the softened butter in a medium sized mixing bowl. Using a cocktail zester, zest the orange directly over the softened butter so that the spray of essential oil will go into the bowl.

If you zest using a microplane, you will not get these essential oils, but if that is the only zesting tool in your kitchen, go ahead and use it knowing your compound butter will be subpar.

Grind the cardamom seeds in a mortar and pestle. Add to the butter with a small pinch of Maldon salt and mix until fully incorporated with a soft rubber spatula.

Add a generous pat of the compound butter to the hot pancakes.

Flannel vegetable hash with poached eggs

Some form of fried potatoes is a critical component to a weekend brunch. If you have left over mashed potatoes from the night before, you can fry them up in a cast iron pan, add some leftover steak, top with a fried egg and call it a day. Or start fresh with a load of veggies from your summer CSA or farmers market for a flannel vegetable hash like below. The variety of vibrant colors from summer vegetables make this a flannel hash with the grated crisscross pattern resembling the bright flannel shirts of my high school days. The vegetables listed below work well, but you can use any combination you find in your kitchen. The description below for poaching eggs is long, but the process itself is actually simple. Don't let them intimidate you.

FLANNEL VEGETABLE HASH

2 potatoes

1 onion

1 zucchini

1 carrot

1 beet

1 Tbsp salt

Grapeseed oil

POACHED EGGS

4 or 5 eggs

1 tsp Maldon salt

Wash all the vegetables. Peel and trim the carrot, onion and beet. Grate all the vegetables using the large grater attachment in a food processor, or with the large holes of a box grater over a large mixing bowl. Mix well and toss with salt. Let sit for 10 minutes and then drain off any collected liquid, squeezing by hand or straining. The more liquid you remove, the crispier the hash will be.

Heat a griddle or cast iron pan to medium and coat with a glug of grapeseed oil. Grab a fistful of veggies, squeeze one last time over the sink and place in the hot oil as a pancake, fitting 3 or 4 in the pan. Pat down to flatten with a metal spatula. Flip after a few minutes, adding another glug of oil and patting down again. After both sides are golden brown and crispy, remove the pancakes from the pan. Serve with a sprinkle of Maldon and two poached eggs per plate.

POACHED EGGS

For poaching eggs, use the freshest eggs available and a delicate touch. Use a pan with about 4 inches of height, filled with at least 2 or 3 inches of water.

Bring water just to a boil, add 1 teaspoon salt, and turn down to a low simmer. Crack an egg and carefully slip it from the shell into the water from as close to the surface as possible. Cook only 4 or 5 eggs at a time so they have room.

Keep an eye on the eggs and the water temperature. After adding the eggs, the water will fall below a simmer, but it should have small bubbles rising to the top again within a minute. Do not allow the water to get so hot that it violently bubbles and breaks the eggs apart. After 3-4 minutes, if the egg white has solidified, you can lift the egg with a slotted spoon halfway out of the water and jiggle it to see if it is done. The egg white should be solid throughout and the yolk should still have some give to it. Unless you like a hard poached egg, in which case let the egg simmer another minute or so until the yolk is firm to the touch.

Remove the eggs from the water and let the excess liquid drain from the slotted spoon before plating. Serve with Maldon salt and freshly ground pepper.

Cubano with melted fontina, roasted pork and sliced pickle

I lived in New York for a few years while attending law school. Even then, the writing was on the wall: my roommate Zabrina and I threw big parties in our little apartment for the public interest law students, complete with tables full of delectable homemade appetizers: crostini with leeks, fennel or sautéed mushrooms, vegetarian sushi, charcuterie platters, eggplant caviar. In a city where kitchens are often decorative or used as storage for your take out containers, the California style dinner parties were unusual, but much more affordable on a student budget.

When we did eat out, we had specific criteria: the food had to be reasonably priced and taste better than what we made at home. Among my favorite New York haunts that fit the bill was Little Havana, a small Cuban restaurant on the edge of SoHo and Chinatown. The mojitos, grilled elote—corn on the cob with cotija cheese—and cubano sandwiches could sustain an evening avoiding study groups like no one's business.

INGREDIENTS

Pork tenderloin, about 1-1½ pounds

3 cloves garlic

1 Tbsp fresh rosemary needles, picked off the thick stem

1 tsp salt

1 Tbsp olive oil

French baguette

Paris ham

Fontina (or Gruyère or Monterey Jack) cheese

Dill pickles or cornichon, thinly sliced lengthwise

Dijon mustard

Butter, softened

To roast the pork tenderloin, make a paste in a mortar and pestle with the garlic cloves, the rosemary and salt. Then combine with olive oil. Slather this oily paste on all sides of the pork tenderloin. Roast on a baking tray at 400°F for 20-40 minutes, depending on the thickness of the tenderloin. The pork will be firm to the touch when done. Allow to cool.

Slice the baguette into thirds to make 3 Cubanos. Cut a thin layer off of the uneven top crusty side to create a flatter surface to butter and cook on. Slice each third in half lengthwise. Turn the bread inside out so what was the crusty outside is now facing the inside of the sandwich.

Butter both flat outsides of each piece of baguette. Thinly slice the ham, pork roast and cheese. Spread Dijon on the crusty inside, then begin layering cheese, meats and pickles, with the cheese slices closest to the bread.

Place the sandwich, one of the buttered sides down, on a hot cast iron pan over medium heat. Cover the sandwich with parchment paper and place a brick or heavy pan on the top to press it down like a panini. Flip after a few minutes when the first buttered side turns crispy and brown. Apply the parchment and heavy object to the second side. When both sides of the bread are golden brown and the cheese is melty, remove from heat and cut in half at a diagonal to serve.

Challah French toast with strawberries, rhubarb and cream

It is a rare treat to indulge in the sweet aspect of brunch as an adult, so its good to seek out those recipes that are true treasures. This French toast recipe is both a special delight and easy to throw together, as long as you happen to have challah, rhubarb and fresh strawberries lying around. Or, since you are more likely to have flour and yeast lying around, you can make the challah from scratch, but then I guess I can't really say the French toast is easy to throw together (although challah is a fairly easy bread to make!)

This is a spring brunch item, when rhubarb and strawberries are in season. Adapt it during other seasons by subbing in whatever fruit is at its peak. Or sauté bananas and sugar in butter if it is winter and the fruit landscape is barren. The cream is likewise adaptable: whole milk yogurt, whipped cream, and clotted cream (or even vanilla ice cream if you want to go crazy) will all work in place of the crème fraîche.

INGREDIENTS

3 stalks rhubarb, cleaned and cut into ½ inch slices

¼ cup sugar

Juice and zest of an orange, or ⅛ cup water

1 pint strawberries, cleaned and cut in halves or quarters

8 oz crème fraîche

2 Tbsp sugar

1 tsp lemon juice

1 challah loaf, sliced

4 eggs

1 cup whole milk

3 Tbsp sugar

1 tsp vanilla

½ tsp salt

In a small saucepan, cook together the rhubarb, ¼ cup sugar, orange juice and zest or water. Let simmer for 5 minutes, stirring occasionally, until the rhubarb softens and turns into a chunky jam-like compote. Let cool.

Prepare the strawberries. If they are perfectly sweet and delicious, let them be. If they are a little rough around the edges, or a little bland because they are from a grocery store rather than a farmers market, toss with a couple spoonfuls of sugar and a pinch of salt and let macerate for a few minutes.

Add the lemon juice and 2 tablespoons sugar to the crème fraîche and whip together until smooth. Taste and add more sugar or lemon juice if desired.

Beat together the eggs, milk, 3 tablespoons sugar, vanilla and salt in a flat bottomed baking dish. Dip each slice of challah into the egg mixture and let sit on each side for 10-30 seconds, depending on how dry the bread is. It should soak up some of the egg mixture but not turn soggy. Let excess egg drip back into the baking dish and set the bread into a hot frying pan with melted butter over medium heat.

Cook two pieces of soaked bread at a time. After a minute or two, when the bottom has browned, flip the bread in the pan, adding another pat of butter. When done, move the French toast from the pan to a warm platter in the oven at 200°F. Wait to dip bread into the egg batter until your pan is ready for the next set to prevent the bread from soaking up too much egg batter. Continue until you run out of egg batter.

Serve the platter of French toast with the compote, strawberries and cream.

Crêpes

Growing up on a rural mountain, we never went out to brunch, but weekends often brought special homemade brunch treats like crêpes. For the six of us hill kids (me, my siblings Mayacamas, Paloma and Val, and our cousins Jesse and Jeremy) crêpes were our favorite extravagance. We sat around the table jockeying for the next hot crêpe as they were made. Sugar and a squeeze of lemon juice rolled up with more sugar sprinkled on top was the filling of choice. As we got older, Jesse became the crêpe master. He had specialized crêpe pans and spatulas, and churned them out for a hungover day-after-festivities brunch for the masses, always served alongside a mountain of crispy bacon.

A heavy-bottomed frying pan, either nonstick or regular, works best for crêpes. The temperature of the stove is critical: hot enough to ensure that the batter adheres to the pan as you tilt it to coat the pan with a thin layer, but not hot enough to burn the butter or the crepe. Use medium heat, but let the pan get hot before cooking. The first crêpe often calls for adjustments—either to the batter texture (add another tablespoon of milk if the first one is too thick) or to the stove temperature.

INGREDIENTS

1 cup milk

1 cup flour

1 tsp salt

1 egg

1 Tbsp melted butter

Sweet or savory filling of choice

Whisk or blend the first four ingredients together until smoothly combined. Then add the melted butter and whisk again until just incorporated. Let the batter sit for an hour in the fridge (or overnight) for a smoother batter.

Heat an 8-inch skillet over medium heat (4 or 5 on my electric stove). Add a pat of butter and swirl so the melted butter coats the bottom of the pain. Lift the pan off the heat, pour ¼ cup of batter into the hot pan and immediately start swirling the pan so the batter runs around coating the entire bottom of the pan. It should be even, thin, and 8 inches in diameter. Immediately return to heat and cook for about 45 seconds, until the bottom has golden brown ridges. Flip with a thin metal spatula and cook for an additional 15 seconds. Either serve immediately with an assortment of jam, syrups, fruits, and spreads, or stack on a plate and serve together after you cook the entire batch.

Apple fritters with powdered sugar

This is another of the nostalgic recipes from special Sundays at home. They were a favorite of my brother Val, and as the only boy in the family (and a sweet one at that) his requests were often heeded.

In the fall, a plethora of apples are ripe over a short period of time. This is an easy but indulgent way to make use of excess fruit. I put apple fritters on the brunch menu occasionally at La Musette, much to the local kids' great delight.

Granny Smiths work well here, but since this provides an outlet for an overflow of crisp autumnal apples, any variety will suffice.

INGREDIENTS

4 apples

Crêpe batter (page 41)

Powdered sugar

Lemon wedge

Maple syrup

Prepare the crêpe batter as directed on page 41.

Peel and core the apples. Slice into thin slivers, ideally a circular cross section looking like a donut, about ¼ inch thick. Crescent shapes are fine too, since they are easier to make (although less cute to serve).

Heat a nonstick cast iron or other pan to medium, and melt a pat of butter to coat the bottom of the pan. Dip apple slices in the batter and add to the melted butter, filling the pan but not crowding it. After 45 seconds or so, when the underside has browned edges, flip with a metal spatula. Cook the other side for 30 seconds and pile onto a plate in a 200°F oven until all the fritters are made. Serve with a sprinkle of powdered sugar and a squeeze of lemon or a drizzle of maple syrup.

Eggs and chard baked in cream

Baked eggs are great when all the usual brunch egg dishes feel overplayed. They are refreshingly uncommon, can be largely prepared in advance, and, of course most importantly, taste delightful! The cream firms up while cooking and absorbs the flavors of garlic and greens, making the entire dish perfect for sopping up with toast.

INGREDIENTS

1 bunch chard

2 stalks green garlic (or 2 cloves garlic)

1 Tbsp butter

6 eggs

½ cup cream or half-and-half

Gruyère cheese

½ tsp salt

Clean and remove the chard leaves from the stems, reserving the stems for some other purpose (perhaps a chard stem gratin or added to fried rice). Blanch greens in salted boiling water for about 45 seconds. Scoop out with a mesh strainer and dunk in ice water to stop the cooking. Gently squeeze the water from the leaves and roughly chop.

Clean and dice the green garlic, using the white and light green parts. Sauté in 1 tablespoon of butter for a minute, and then add the chard and sauté for another 30 seconds.

Transfer to a ceramic oven-proof 8- or 10-inch round cazuela or baking dish and spread out evenly. Add the cream or half-and-half and then gently crack the eggs into the dish. The eggs should be mostly submerged by the liquid. Add more dairy if necessary. Salt and add a layer of grated gruyère on top.

Bake in a 400°F oven for 13 minutes until the eggs have set. Serve with a side of toast.

CHAPTER 3:

HARVEST AT SKY VINEYARDS

CHAPTER 3:
Harvest at Sky Vineyards

I was born and raised on Mt. Veeder, the crown overlooking Napa's wine country. My grandparents bought land in the early 1970s to help support my father's dream of growing grapes and making wine. My parents and their friends christened the land Sky Vineyards and cleared 12 acres to plant Zinfandel. My grandfather Walter, an architect and Frank Lloyd Wright disciple, designed, and with my father Lore, built a barn as the winery. My uncles helped my father build a charming but ultra-rustic cabin. And it was in a woodfire-heated corner with no indoor plumbing or electricity that I was born and raised. (They did let me roam beyond that corner, and we got indoor plumbing when I was 7, and solar electricity when I was 13). My siblings, cousins and I roamed the mountain top as half-feral beasts who were often conscripted into gardening, cooking, homesteading, grape-growing and winemaking duties.

In the first era of Sky, with Lore at the helm, my grandparents brought their architect and birder friends up to help harvest. In later eras, my sister's viticulture friends or my law school buddies comprised the volunteer crew. And through generations, the endeavor continued as we labored at small-scale farming and winemaking surrounded by the helping hands of family and friends.

Integral to this collaborative process was an inescapable commitment to hosting our family and friends in our home with overflowing wine and food. Harvest dinners were prepared with the bounty of local farms or our garden, cooked over an open fire, and served out on the picnic tables to the collected ten or forty friends who converged to help. And through the labor, the feasting, the stargazing, and the wine-fortified laughter, generations of community were forged.

It was this concept of community that I brought with me to Niwot and that informed my vision of what La Musette could be. My menu has always been influenced by the California food and wine scene, and many of my dishes have origins in the harvest meals at Sky Vineyards.

Sky Zinfandel braised duck legs with cherries and star anise

Given my undying love of duck legs, they headlined many special dinners at Sky and often made an appearance on the La Musette rotating menus. One of my early culinary influences and perhaps the origin of my duck obsession was Chef Lauren Lyle of the Bay Wolf restaurant in Oakland. Lauren was part of the Sky crew for a spell and would cook amazing meals that often relied on the tub of duck fat that she always had on hand. She is the co-author of one of my favorite cookbooks, the Bay Wolf Restaurant Cookbook, which boasts 16 different duck recipes!

Duck meat is rich and flavorful. It is perfectly suited to integrate seamlessly with its cooking environment, so it is the ideal subject for braising. You can change the braising profile with an almost infinite variety of soffrito, spices, and braising liquids. I love the combination of sweet cherries and spicy star anise here.

INGREDIENTS

4-6 duck legs (always with thigh attached)

1 onion, diced

1 small fennel bulb, diced

1 carrot, diced

1 leek, diced

½ cup fresh cherries, cut in half and pitted, or ⅓ cup dried cherries

2 star anise

1 cardamom pod

2 cups red wine, preferably Sky Zinfandel

2 cups chicken broth

Salt and pepper

1-4 cups duck fat

Salt and pepper both sides of the duck legs, preferably several hours before cooking. In a heavy bottomed dutch oven or braising pan, add a tablespoon of duck fat. Add the duck legs, skin side down, and sear for about five minutes until browned. Remove and let rest on a plate.

Add the diced onion to the duck fat in the pan, salt and sauté. Once the onion has softened, add the diced fennel, and then carrots, and then leeks, sautéing for a few minutes in between each addition. The vegetables should start to turn translucent but not brown. Turn down the heat if they are browning or add another dollop of duck fat if they look too dry.

Add the cherries, star anise and cardamom. Add the duck legs back to the pan, nestled on the cooked vegetables, skin side up, along with any juices accumulated on the plate. Deglaze the pan by pouring wine in and scraping any brown fond sticking to the bottom of the pan to ensure those flavorful bits get dislodged and incorporated into the braising liquid. Pour the chicken broth over the duck legs until they are almost submerged with only the skin remaining above the liquid's surface.

Wrap aluminum foil over the pan and secure tightly with the lid to prevent evaporated braising liquid from escaping. It is the continual process of liquid evaporating, condensing on the lid and then dripping back onto the meat in a more concentrated form that creates the braising magic.

Braise in a 350ºF oven for 90 minutes. After 90 minutes, remove from the oven and check. The duck legs should be meltingly tender. If most of the liquid has evaporated, you can add another ½ cup of chicken stock to hydrate it. Return to the oven to cook for an additional 10 minutes uncovered to crisp the duck skin.

Serve with a spoonful of the reduced cooking liquid atop the legs.

Duck confit

Duck reigns supreme in Skyla's meat hierarchy. Few things surpass a perfectly cooked duck leg. It beats a crispy porchetta, a braised short rib, a marbled thick grilled ribeye, and even a silky boudin blanc sausage. Selecting between a Zinfandel braised duck leg and a crispy duck confit is like choosing which member of BTS is my bias. Low and slow are the watch words for duck. When roasting or confiting, go for a gentle temperature and extended cook time to achieve the falling-off-the-bone tenderness that melts the duck fat into the meat.

A sublime bonus of making duck confit is the excess duck fat remaining after the meat is consumed, which should be strained and preserved for other uses. Such other uses may include: sautéing turnips, frying parboiled potatoes, dolling up a baked potato or rice, frying eggs, making cassoulet, or just starting a new batch of duck confit.

INGREDIENTS

8 duck legs

At least 2 cups duck fat

Fresh thyme

Bay leaves

1 head garlic

Generously salt and sprinkle both sides of the duck legs with crumbled bay leaves and thyme leaves. Let sit in the fridge overnight and covered, if time permits.

Slice the garlic head in half and place both halves in a baking dish that will snugly accommodate all the legs. Strew two bay leaves and several sprigs of thyme around the bottom of the pan. Add the duck fat and place the pan in the oven for a couple minutes to liquify the fat. Tuck the duck legs into the fat, skin side up, submerging them at least halfway or three quarters of the way up the legs. The legs will render more fat through the cooking process so it's fine if they are only partially submerged. Cover tightly with foil.

Cook in a 200°F oven for 4 hours. The meat should start to detach from the bone and seem loose if you shake the leg from the protruding bone. If not using immediately, let the legs cool in the fat a bit, and then transfer to a large glass container. Strain the herbs and garlic out and pour the fat to cover the legs entirely. If covered entirely with fat, the legs will keep in the fridge for months. If any of the meat is exposed, however, use it within a week.

To serve, crisp the skin by heating for five minutes skin-side down on a hot cast iron pan, or on a sheet in the oven on 400°F for a few minutes.

Steak with chimichurri

Grilled meat paired with several vegetable sides and a bright herbaceous chimichurri sauce is the height of outdoor summer dining.

My preference when craving steak is always a thick bone-in ribeye. When that is cost-prohibitive, I tend toward skirt and flatiron. Likewise, open flames with a wood fire makes the best steak, but for convenience's sake, sometimes a charcoal fire or a gas grill are your best bets. If nothing else, a cast iron pan on a stove will work.

INGREDIENTS

Steak

Salt

Pepper

CHIMICHURRI SAUCE

¼-½ cup of chiffonaded fresh herbs of any combination: Italian parsley, basil, oregano, thyme, cilantro, tarragon, sage and/or chervil, but go easy on the stronger herbs like sage and tarragon

1 medium shallot, minced and salted

1 Tbsp each of minced umami ingredients, solo or in combination: anchovy filets, preserved lemon, lemon zest, olives

¼-½ cup olive oil

Take the steak out of the fridge ½-1 hour before grilling and generously salt and pepper both sides. Do not over-salt a thin steak. When the grill is quite hot, throw the steaks on and let sear untouched for 3-5 minutes, depending on the thickness. There should be nice char marks from the grill and a nice golden caramelized crust forming. Sear the second side for 3-5 minutes. If needed, reduce the heat slightly and cook an additional minute or two on each side. Test the steak by quickly depressing it with a finger. For rare or medium rare, the steak should have some cushion action when depressed. For medium well, it should be firmer. When the steak feels right, remove from the grill and rest for five minutes on a plate.

The steak will continue to cook while it rests. Slice the steak against the grain and pour any collected juices back on top just before serving.

For the chimichurri, add all the ingredients together in a bowl and cover with the olive oil. The olive oil should rise above the herbs by ¼-½ inch. If covered in oil, the chimichurri will last a few days in the fridge and you can easily add an additional ¼ cup olive oil if necessary. Leftovers will zhuzh up sandwiches, hardboiled or fried eggs, greens, or potato salads.

Serve the steak on a platter dressed with a generous drizzle of chimichurri and additional sauce on the side.

Shrimp wrapped in bacon

My college friend's ex-high school boyfriend moved to California for grad school and became a fixture of the Sky Crew. Don Baron is now one of my closest friends, officiated the marriage of my brother, and brings his kids to harvest as part of the next generation of Sky Crew. In our post-college days, he could always be counted on to bring shrimp or scallops to wrap in bacon and throw on the grill for every Sky gathering. If you eat shellfish and pork, this is a failure-proof party favorite. For many of the private special events La Musette hosted at the Wheel House, the shrimp wrapped in bacon rarely made it to the appetizer table as guests mobbed the server walking the platter through the bar.

Clean, shell and devein the shrimp. While deveining, slice into the back generously so they butterfly out when they cook. Clean and pat dry with paper towels. If using sea scallops, rinse and pat dry.

Toss the seafood with a couple spoonfuls of spicy chili crunch and a generous pinch of salt. Alternatively, a sprinkle of salt and chili flakes will suffice.

Wrap each shrimp or scallop in half of a strip of bacon and secure with a toothpick. Grill on high heat over fire, charcoal or a gas grill. Flip after a couple minutes. The bacon should be crispy and the shellfish cooked through. Because the bacon will drip fat over the flames, close the grill while cooking or have a spray bottle of water available to squelch the flames.

Alternatively, place the shellfish wrapped in bacon on a rack on a baking sheet and bake at 450°F for about 7 minutes or until the bacon is cooked.

INGREDIENTS

- 1 pound large shrimp (15/16 count) or sea scallops (the big ones!)
- 1 pound bacon
- Spicy chili crunch sauce (I like Denver-based Kream Kimchi, Lao Gan Ma, or Momofuku brands)
- Salt
- Toothpicks

Harvest green salad

Almost every harvest meal at Sky featured a green salad in addition to anything else being served. At La Musette, I likewise usually offered a green salad with various toppings and rotating vinaigrettes. Use whatever salad greens are available from the local farmers or whatever lettuces look most vivacious. The vinaigrette below is my base recipe and can be altered with the addition of different herbs or different vinegars to fit whatever salad is on the table.

Dress the whole salad just before eating. Start with less dressing than you think you need and only add more after mixing thoroughly and tasting a piece of lettuce. Overdressed salads are the worst. Also, make sure that your lettuce is as dry as possible. Water-logged salads are actually way worse than overdressed salads.

To compose a harvest salad, prepare a well-curated assortment of vegetables and other ingredients, with contrasting textures, complementary flavors, and protein if necessary. Sometimes a fruit component is nice, but stick to one variety and consider matching it with a cheese and a nut rather than other vegetables.

Place the minced shallot in a glass pint canning jar and add sugar and salt. Let sit for a few minutes so the salt and sugar macerate the shallot and mellow it out. Add the mustard and the vinegars and let sit for another few minutes. Then add the olive oil, screw the lid on, and shake vigorously to make an emulsion. For a larger batch, add up to ½ cup of vinegar and oil each without having to increase the other ingredients. If you like a more or less acidic dressing, adjust the proportion accordingly.

Assemble the salad and toss, conservatively to start, with the dressing. Add a pinch of salt and pepper. If all the guts have fallen to the bottom (the non-lettuce ingredients), scoop some out and spread on top of the salad so it looks pretty. Alternatively, if you are using a nut, a seed, and/ or a cheese, you can add these after dressing the rest of the salad as they don't need the dressing and will look nice on top.

INGREDIENTS

Garden lettuces

Vegetables:

- avocado; lemon or Armenian cucumbers; fennel; watermelon radish; carrots; bell peppers; sliced snap peas; cherry tomatoes, halved; roasted cauliflower, in small florets; roasted beets; fava beans; steamed green beans, sliced on the bias

Fruits:

- perfectly ripe pear or apple slices; orange or grapefruit supremes (all the pith removed); pomegranate seeds; grilled peaches

Crunch:

- toasted almonds, macadamia nuts, pine nuts, walnuts, pecans, hazelnuts; toasted pumpkin seeds (pepitas); toasted sunflower seeds; fried shallots

Protein:

- fresh goat cheese; blue cheese; thinly sliced Parmesan; Vella's dry jack; cotija; ricotta salata; fresh mozzarella or burrata; beans

VINAIGRETTE

1 small shallot, minced

1 tsp sugar

½ tsp salt

1 tsp dijon mustard

1 Tbsp rice vinegar

1 Tbsp sherry vinegar

1 Tbsp champagne vinegar

3 Tbsp olive oil

Amy's harvest paella

One of my favorite nights of the year is when Amy, my father's partner, makes harvest paella. She starts three days in advance, shopping at Monterey Fish and the farmers markets for the best local seafood and produce; making a stock with fish bones, shrimp carcasses, perhaps some lobster shells; taking fresh cranberry beans out of their pods; cooking each ingredient that needs extra attention separately.

Sky Crew volunteers reminisce about Amy Paellas of Harvests Past: some remember the year of the dazzling squid ink paella; others remember when that one "volunteer" skimped on work, drank all the Pliny and scraped lobster off more than her share of the paella; others recall the year we went through so much aioli that Amy paused mid-dinner to whip up another heaping bowlful.

The main event—after grapes are picked and crushed, buckets and boxes are cleaned, fermenters of nascent wine are punched down—is Amy assembling and cooking the paella over an open fire in the backyard. Many of the 20 or 30 friends and family gather around, wine glasses full, eyes blurry from the satisfying exhaustion of a full day of harvesting, jovially watching with anticipation as Amy layers flavors and textures expertly in the enormous paella pans.

And then the picnic tables are full of the dulcet sounds of plating and imbibing, with dinner a little quieter than the usual rambunctious revelry as the group savors the perfect combination of flavor-soaked Bomba rice and morsels of perfectly cooked fish, mussels, shrimp and squid, topped with fresh aioli.

Having said all that, the recipe below is not in fact Amy's paella. It is my abbreviated version, inspired by the hallowed memories of harvest paellas, and served at La Museet for Niwot's Around the World Day.

This recipe is for a 15- or 17-inch paella pan, feeding 4-6 people. I have used a cast iron pan when needed as a substitute. The key to scaling the paella size up or down is to maintain a 4:1 ratio of stock:rice.

INGREDIENTS

1 pound large shrimp (15/16 count), with shells and heads on

1 pound mussels

1 pound white fish like halibut or snapper

½ pound squid, pre-cleaned

8 oz cured Spanish chorizo

1 onion

1 red bell pepper

1 fennel bulb

1 pound fresh English peas

1 pound bag dried cranberry or Corona beans from Rancho Gordo

2 cups Bomba Spanish rice

Olive oil

Salt

Pepper

Smoked Paprika

1-2 Tbsp chili crunch (optional)

1 bay leaf

1 garlic clove

Amy's harvest paella

Soak the dried beans overnight in plenty of water. Cook in the soaking water over medium heat with 2 teaspoons salt, a bay leaf, a whole garlic clove, and 2 tablespoons olive oil for about 45 minutes, or until soft enough to eat. Corona beans will take longer. Alternatively, substitute with a jar of cooked large white beans, rinsed, preferable from a glass jar rather than a can.

In a large pot with at least 10 cups of water, make the stock with all of the trimmings from the other ingredients: heads and shells from the shrimp, any trimmings from the fish, trimmings from the onion and fennel, 2 tablespoons salt. Simmer on low for 2-4 hours. Strain.

While the stock and beans are cooking, prepare all of the other ingredients. Dice the onions, fennel and bell pepper into similarly sized small cubes. Dice the chorizo into small cubes. Remove the English peas from their pods. Clean the shrimp, removing the dark intestine from the back and cutting about a third of the way into the shrimp backs so the shrimp butterfly while cooked. Salt the shrimp and toss with chili crunch. Soak the mussels in cold salt water to remove sand, scrub if needed, and remove any beards. Cut the fish into bite-size pieces. Slice the squid into rings about 1/2 inch thick.

When ready to assemble and cook the paella, 45-60 minutes before serving, heat the paella pan over a wood burning fire with a generous bed of hot coals, or over a propane burner. Add a glug of olive oil and toss the shrimp in when the oil is sizzling hot. Cook for a couple minutes, tossing occasionally until the shrimp are just cooked and have lost their translucence. Add the squid in with the shrimp for the last minute of cooking. Remove the shrimp and squid from the pan and reserve. Add the diced onions, bell peppers, fennel, paprika, and 1 tablespoon salt to the hot shrimp oil. Sauté until the onions have turned translucent. Add the diced chorizo and sauté for another 30 seconds.

Pour 8 cups of the shrimp stock into the paella pan and bring to a boil. As soon as it boils, sprinkle the Bomba rice evenly over the pan. Let the paella simmer for about 10-15 minutes until the rice has evaporated much of the liquid and the rice is starting to look plump, but there is still about ¼-inch of stock in the rice. Sprinkle the peas and beans throughout the paella, then nestle the fish and mussels into the rice. Continue cooking until the liquid has been absorbed and the mussels have opened. The rice should be almost fully cooked through, with just a slight bite. You can add another cup of the stock if the rice is not close to done. Strew the cooked shrimp and squid over the paella. Remove from heat and cover with a clean damp linen kitchen towel. Let sit for 10 minutes to continue steaming and finish cooking the rice.

Serve with a bowl of aioli and a vinegary salad.

CHAPTER 4:
OLDS FAMILY TRADITIONS

CHAPTER 4
Olds Family Traditions

I had a childhood bifurcated by my parents divorcing when I was three years old. I lived in two households, located in close proximity on a rural mountaintop but legions apart in terms of temperament, philosophy, culture, and society. Perhaps the only commonality was a commitment to communing over cooking and eating together.

The households alternated or doubled up on holidays, with family traditions on each side deeply ingrained and always centered around food. Thanksgiving lunch at my paternal grandparents' house had a coursed menu (chestnut soup and orange rolls; turkey, mashed potatoes, stuffing, two types of cranberry sauces; multiple pies) and if one dish deviated from tradition, all hell would break loose. One year an aunt convinced my grandmother to make brioche (the Christmas tradition) instead of orange rolls and, well, nearly forty years later, the audacity and wrongness is still on my mind. Friday Thanksgiving Dinner was at my maternal grandmother's house. Everyone brought a dish and always the same dish: crab cocktail from Aunt Carroll, buttered carrots from Uncle Jerry; Grandma's Parker House Rolls, the can of jellied cranberry from Uncle Ron, and so forth.

As I started my own household, I added new traditions while carrying on the old ones. An additional Friendsgiving dinner with champagne, Dungeness crab and miso soup following the usual family lunch. The traditions become so ingrained that it is hard to separate the menu from the occasion. If I do not eat orange rolls, it is not Thanksgiving.

My concept of family culinary traditions extends beyond the dishes that are so linked to the holidays and special occasions. Sometimes a tradition develops when someone makes and brings a signature dish over and over again, to everyone's great delight. That food becomes linked to the identity of the person and their role in the community. By enjoying, expecting, adopting and including that food, you are expressing your love and acceptance of the person who shares it. Amy's eggnog, Don Baron's shrimp wrapped in bacon, Edna's Seven Layer Dip, the Briner family coleslaw, Aunt Diane's Brownies, Matt's mom's stuffing, Mica's soft salted chocolate chip cookies, Melanie's strawberry and cream birthday cake, Pickle's goose fixins, Joyce's mom's roast duck. When I make someone's family recipe, I am remembering, honoring, missing, and loving them.

The forging of new culinary traditions cements the bonds of friendship and kinship. Wherever I go, I like to share and build those bonds. So now, there is a new cadre of families in Boulder and Niwot who understand that Thanksgiving means orange rolls.

Grandma Olds's orange rolls

Grandma Olds's orange rolls are the holy grail of my culinary existence. They are a family treasure that activates memories of cherished meals stretching back through my entire life, imbued with the essence of both Olds grandparents, and regularly shared with new family and friends as an expression of love.

These rolls have sweet and zesty orange butter twirled through a light and pillowy dough. They could be served for brunch but we eat them with chestnut or squash soup as our first course for our Thanksgiving feast. My niece and nephew, Dakota and Archer, greet them with the same sparkle in their eyes that I sported as a young child.

*Be prepared for a total of 6 hours of dough rising

INGREDIENTS

1 cup milk

2 Tbsp butter

1 Tbsp yeast

½ tsp salt

3 eggs, beaten well

½ cup sugar

4 cups flour

½ cup softened butter

2 oranges for zesting

½ cup sugar

Scald the milk in a small pot, heating it to just under a boil, around 180°F, and remove from heat. Add the butter and stir until melted. Let the mixture cool for a few minutes to about 110°F and then sprinkle the yeast over it. After letting the yeast activate and begin to bubble, add the salt, eggs, sugar, and 1 cup of the flour, mixing well after each addition.

Let the dough rise for two hours covered with a clean kitchen towel. Add the remaining 3 cups of flour. Mix well to incorporate but do not knead. Allow to rise for another two hours.

Make the filling by zesting the orange rind directly over the softened butter with the zester pictured on page 34 so the essential oils from the peel coat the butter. Add the sugar and mix with a rubber spatula until fully incorporated.

After the dough has risen the second time, roll it into a large rectangle, about 12 x 16 inches. Using the rubber spatula, spread the orange butter over the entire surface up to the edges. Roll the dough into a log lengthwise so you will have a 16-inch long roll. Cut into 12 pieces and place on a buttered high-sided sheet cake pan, spiral side facing up. Cover with plastic wrap and let rise for an additional two hours. Alternatively, refrigerate and let rise overnight, allowing to come to room temperature 1 hour before baking.

Bake for 20 mins at 375°F. Serve rolls upside down and warm.

Matt's mom's fennel and sausage stuffing

I love collecting recipes from people. Sharing a meaningful recipe affords an intimate glimpse into who and why they are. When I worked as a defense attorney for capital appeals, sometimes my client's family was generous enough to share a recipe that was a childhood or birthday favorite of my client. You understand something new when you record and recreate someone's favorite family recipe. It shows how we are shaped by the food we grow up with and how food, taste, identity and memory are intertwined.

In creating new family traditions and carrying on the next generation of holiday meals, I have endeavored to include the family dishes of the in-laws and the exes. This recipe is adapted from Barbara Gerloff, the mother of my longtime but now ex-partner Matt. After decades of Thanksgivings with the Gerloff sausage stuffing, this is now cemented as a part of my Thanksgiving meal.

INGREDIENTS

2 Tbsp duck fat

1 large yellow onion, peeled, trimmed and diced

1 fennel bulb, cleaned, trimmed and diced

1 pound bulk (or casing removed) pork sausage from the butcher (sweet Italian, garlic, or breakfast sausage)

1 apple or quince, peeled, cored and diced

¼ cup chestnuts, cooked, peeled and chopped (optional)

1 loaf challah or other soft bread, cut into cubes

2 cups chicken stock, preferably homemade

1 Tbsp fresh sage, chiffonaded

2 Tbsp fresh thyme, de-stemmed and minced

1 Tbsp salt

1 tsp freshly ground black pepper

Heat the duck fat in a skillet. Add the onions and sauté with a pinch of salt until translucent. Add the fennel and continue to sauté for a few minutes. Add the pork sausage and break up into bite size pieces with a flat edged wooden spoon while sautéing. Add the apple or quince and sauté another 2 minutes. Add the chestnuts. Remove from heat.

In a large mixing bowl, soak the cubes of bread in the chicken stock. Add the salt, pepper and fresh herbs. Toss the sautéed ingredients from the skillet in with the soggy bread and mix together thoroughly. Move the stuffing to a glass baking dish (or fill a chicken/duck/turkey cavity if you have a bird and prefer traditionally cooked stuffing). Bake at 350ºF for 25 minutes until browned.

Easter blintzes

Cheese blintzes are the quintessential Olds family Easter brunch fare. We served blintzes with a dollop of sour cream, a sprinkle of cinnamon, and cherry or apricot preserves, accompanied by a long-standing debate over the correct order of those condiments. Fruit salad and Canadian bacon came on the side, and the homemade fizzy apple cider was accompanied by a long-standing debate of whether Grandma forgot the honey in the cider-making that year.

The blintzes recipe initially came from the Rhoades family, Berkeley neighbors of my grandparents in the 1960s. No one knows how this became our holiday tradition, but blintzes now define Easter for me.

INGREDIENTS

Crêpe recipe
(page 41), doubled

CHEESE FILLING

2 pounds farmers cheese (or fresh ricotta or cottage cheese, strained in cheese cloth)

⅓ cup sugar

¾ cup half-and-half

4 egg yolks

2 Tbsp orange zest

¼ tsp salt

Combine all the cheese filling ingredients and fold together with a rubber spatula until fully incorporated.

Prepare crêpes according to the recipe on page 41, but only cook one side of the crêpe, removing after the first side is done. Stack on a plate.

Fill each crepe with a shy ¼ cup of filling, placed in the center of the undercooked side of the crêpe. Fold like an envelope so you have a 2-3-inch square pocket. Place on a buttered cooking sheet with the folded side down. A dozen blintzes should fit on a large tray, or place 6 envelopes each on 2 smaller baking sheets.

Bake at 350°F for 35-40 minutes.

Serve with a dollop of sour cream, a dollop of jam (preferable cherry or apricot) and a dusting of cinnamon.

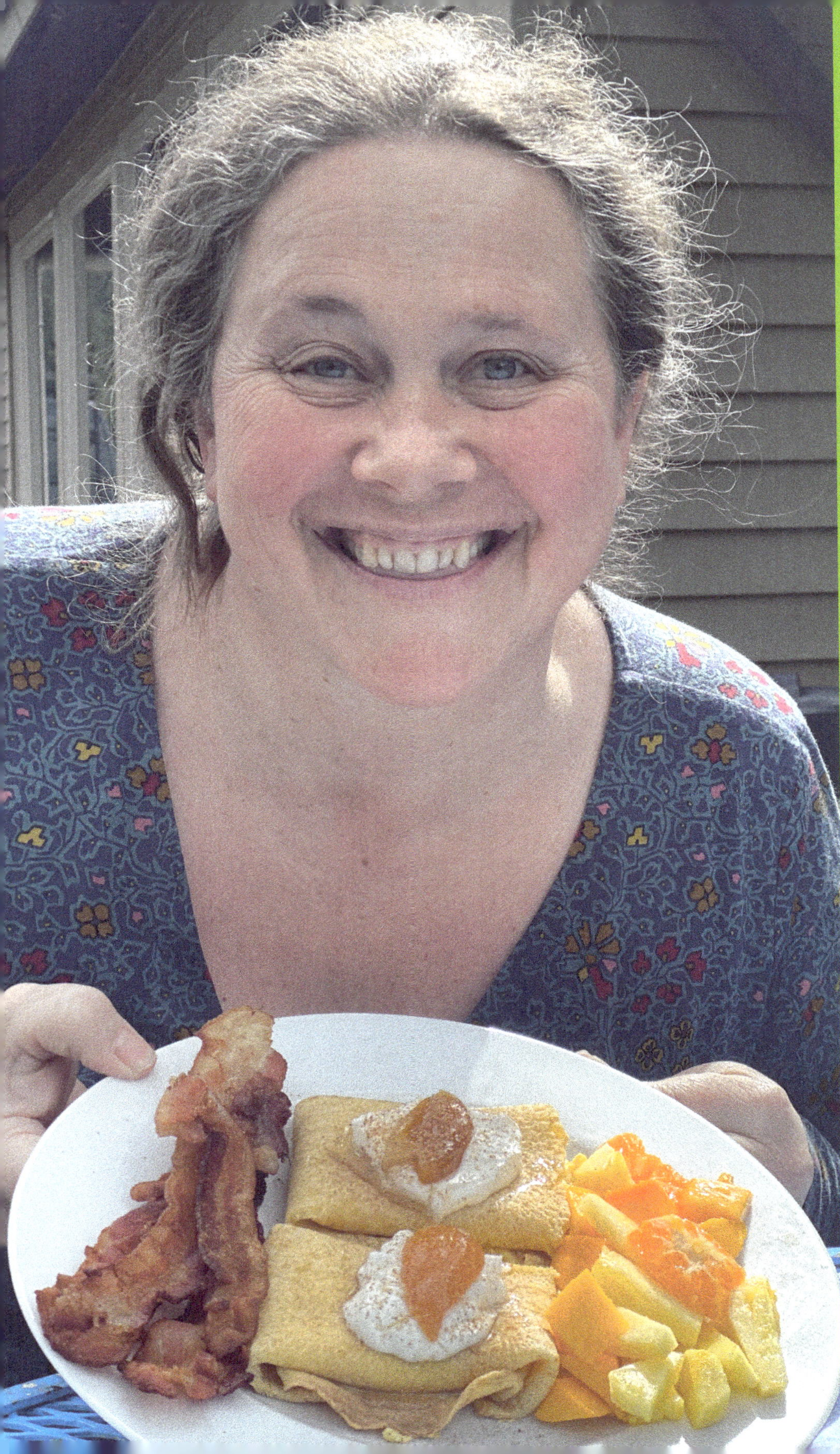

Lore's bouillabaisse

My father Lore...well, stories and descriptions of him could fill an entire book, but he is rarely in the kitchen as dinner is being prepared. When I was younger he had a few signature dishes that he would bust out for special occasions. His bouillabaisse was one such dish, usually making an appearance for my sister's January birthday. Lore's bouillabaisse is a cream and potato fish stew served with a garlicky aioli or rouille. He refuses to make it now that his partner Amy is the chef at Chez Panisse Restaurant, but it lives on in our memories. My adaptation is based on those memories (because of course if you asked him for his recipe, he would claim not to remember how to make it or possibly deny that it ever existed, while still asking Amy to make it for him).

INGREDIENTS

Fish bones

1 pound white fish like halibut, snapper, hake or cod

1 onion, diced, with skin and ends reserved for the stock

1 leek, diced, with the green parts reserved for the stock

1 fennel frond, diced, with the greens reserved for the stock

1 large carrot, diced, with the peels reserved for the stock

2 large yukon gold potatoes, peeled and cubed

1 bottle clam juice

½ cup white wine, preferably from a sea adjacent wine region

1 pound large shrimp (15/16 count), peeled, deveined and butterflied, with shells reserved for the stock

4-8 sea scallops (the big ones!)

1 pound mussels, rinsed well and debearded

1 loaf sourdough bread

3 cloves garlic

1 serrano pepper

½ cup heavy cream (optional)

Olive oil

Salt

pepper

Make a fish stock by simmering fish bones, shrimp peels, 1 tablespoon salt, and the discards of the onion, leek, fennel and carrot in a large pot of water for a couple hours. Strain and dispose of the solids.

In a heavy-bottomed large pot, sauté the diced onion with a teaspoon of salt in a generous glug of olive oil. After the onion becomes translucent, add the diced leek, fennel and carrot, one ingredient at a time, sautéing for a minute between each addition. Add the potatoes. Deglaze the pan with the white wine, scraping any brown fond off the bottom of the pan into the liquid. Cook for a couple minutes, and then add the claim juice and at least 8 cups of fish stock. Bring to a low boil and simmer until the potato pieces are soft enough to pierce with a fork.

Meanwhile, prepare the seafood and rouille. Cut the fish into 2-inch pieces. Clean the mussels and scallops. Assemble the rouille with a mortar and pestle: deseed the serrano pepper and roughly chop; pound together the garlic cloves and serrano with ½ teaspoon salt until it forms a smooth paste; take two pieces of sourdough bread and dip them briefly into the cooking stew so they are soft but not dripping wet; add to the mortar with a tablespoon of olive oil and pound together with the garlic paste into a spread.

Slice and toast the remaining bread while finishing the stew. Add the seafood to the stew based on size and pay close attention to each ingredient. This step of cooking the seafood is delicate: ensure the cooking is gentle, turning down heat if necessary, and if one type of seafood cooks through faster than expected, remove it temporarily from the stew so it does not overcook. For thick pieces of fish, allot 4 minutes of cook time. After one minute, add the shrimp. After another minute, add the mussels and cover the stew. Add the scallops for the final minute of cooking. Add ½ cup heavy cream, bring back up to piping hot, just under a boil, and taste one last time for saltiness.

To serve, ensure that each bowl has all the seafood components and top with a dollop of rouille and sprinkle of freshly ground pepper. Serve the toasted bread drizzled with olive oil on the side with extra rouille available to spread on the toast or add to the stew.

Paloma's pickled vegetables

My younger sister Paloma has worked for decades in professional kitchens and was a tremendous and frequent guest chef in the food truck. I have learned so much from her and have benefitted from countless hours of her hard work, but more importantly, we always have a raucous fun time cooking together. She also texts me every other month asking me to resend her own pickle recipe.

Below is Paloma's often-requested original pickled vegetable recipe. This recipe is great for all sorts of vegetables and is highly adaptable. I often tweak the spice blend to complement whatever I'm pickling or the menu the pickles support. Common variations may include a bay leaf, juniper or allspice berries, fresh dill, garlic cloves or sliced jalapeños, depending on the desired flavor profile.

INGREDIENTS

2 cups water

2 cups white distilled vinegar

¼ cup red wine or champagne vinegar

2 Tbsp salt

1 Tbsp sugar

1 tsp black peppercorns

1 tsp fennel seeds

1 tsp whole coriander seeds

Vegetables, cleaned, peeled, and thinly sliced, of any combination you desire, such as:

- Onions
- Cauliflower (cut into small florets)
- Carrots
- Tokyo turnips
- Fennel
- Colrahbi
- Beets

Combine all the brining ingredients in a pot and bring to a boil to dissolve the salt and sugar. Turn off the heat and let the spices steep in the brine as you prepare the vegetables. Once the vegetables are prepared, bring the brine back up to a boil and pour over the vegetables, straining the spices out as you pour. Place parchment paper over the submerged veggies and weigh down with a bowl or plate for an hour.

Pickles will last in a closed container submerged in the brine for a couple weeks in the fridge.

Grandma Apgar's gado gado

My maternal grandmother was a bit of an enigma. She was a constant in my childhood, living on the same ranch right next door, funding and accompanying us on family trips, but she was not a soft or nurturing woman. She disliked the rambunctiousness of the six grandchildren constantly around and had esoteric interests. We became closer when I was an older teenager, but I missed out on knowing her as an adult. For most of my youth, she had a Coke and a cigarette in one hand and Jeopardy on in the background. Among her unexpected interests was an intense focus on Indonesia, manifesting in her sartorial choices, some dabbling with obscure religion, and the appearance of an occasional Indonesian dish on the table besides her usual Mac 'n cheese and white bread.

The Indonesian dish I most associate with her is gado gado, a vegetarian platter with peanut sauce. She would break it out for parties as an appetizer tray: boiled eggs and steamed vegetables with the spicy coconut milk and peanut butter dipping sauce, which was quite exotic for Sonoma in the 1980s. Thirty years later, when traveling in Malaysia with the Yee family, I came across gado gado again at a casual lunch spot in the town of Miri on the island of Borneo. Of course I ordered it and was transported back to Grandma Apgar's kitchen. The Malaysian dish was served more as a salad, doused with a thin and spicy peanut dressing, replete with steamed vegetables and seared tempeh. I loved it. So of course I adapted it and served it at La Musette.

INGREDIENTS

- 3 red potatoes
- ½ pounds green beans, trimmed
- ½ head cauliflower
- 3 eggs, hard boiled, peeled and quartered
- 2 carrots, peeled
- 2 Armenian cucumbers
- 1 bell pepper
- Tempeh or pressed tofu

PEANUT DRESSING

- ½ inch fresh ginger, peeled and minced
- 1-2 garlic cloves, peeled and minced
- ½ jalapeño, minced
- 2 Tbsp sesame oil

(Anytime sesame oil is called for in this book, I use toasted sesame oil.)

- 1 cup peanut butter
- ½ cup coconut milk
- 1 tsp ketjap manis (or 1 tsp fish sauce + 1 tsp soy sauce)
- 1 lemon
- Water

Clean and slice the vegetables into bite-sized pieces. Steam potatoes, green beans, cauliflower and carrots until pierceable by a fork, but not mushy. Each vegetable will take a different length of time, but begin checking after 5 minutes. Transfer each vegetable from the steamer into an ice bath for a few minutes to stop the cooking process and chill the vegetables. Set aside to dry.

Slice the cucumbers and bell peppers, leaving them raw. Sear tempeh in sesame oil for a few minutes per side, if using, and then cut into bite-size pieces. The pressed tofu can be sliced cold, or heated if preferred.

To make the dressing, sauté the ginger, garlic and jalapeño in 2 tablespoons sesame oil for about 30 seconds. Add the peanut butter, coconut milk and ketjap manis and stir. Drizzle water in as you stir to create a smooth and pourable consistency. This will use between ¼-1 cup of water, depending on the consistency of the peanut butter. Add the juice of the lemon. Let simmer for about 5 minutes. Adjust the consistency with additional water if necessary. If the dressing breaks, transfer to a blender and add a little more water to emulsify.

Serve vegetables in a shallow bowl with dressing poured on top, or as an appetizer tray with a bowl of the peanut sauce. Adorn with the boiled eggs.

COMFORTING ITALIAN FARE

CHAPTER 5:
Comforting Italian Fare

When I was a junior at Wellesley College, I tried to study abroad in France but ended up in Florence. I had been in Italy for a few days with a family camping trip when I was 13 and remembered how I was instantly awestruck by a passionate love for the place. This happens every time I find myself in Italy. The food, the language, the wine, the landscape, the architecture, the art, the weight of the air. Two weeks into the study abroad program, I was ready to change my life. I realized a semester there was insufficient, so I started taking intensive classes to transfer to the year-long program. I abandoned my minor in math to instead double major with Italian and immersed myself in the culture. I was in love—with the language, the art, the buildings, the contours of the land, and, of course, the cuisine. The same fundamentals I knew from Californian cuisine—quality local and seasonal ingredients simply prepared—were showcased in every town as a basic rubric of life.

Living in Florence as a 21-year-old, I started really learning to cook. I had been baking since I was young, but the ingredients and food culture of Italy catapulted me into this life-long love affair with pasta, braised and cured meats, cheeses, bitter chicories, basil, and olive oil.

I learned about insaporire, the verb meaning "to infuse with flavor" and describing the fundamental technique of building a dish by layering ingredients. This technique and its philosophy inform how I approach both cooking and life in general. Insaporire begins with olive oil in a hot pan, to which you add diced onions and always a pinch of salt. Then you watch, listen, and inhale the aromas to decide when to add the next ingredient. Each successive ingredient is added at the right moment and given the proper time to change and develop.

All your senses are engaged as you add layer upon layer. It requires patience, effort, focus, discernment and trust that things will develop as they should. And, at the end, the resultant whole is greater than the sum of its parts.

The recipes that follow are my comfort food. They are dishes I make for myself and my friends over and over again.

Bolognese lasagna

This bolognese lasagna is perhaps my signature dish, the one that friends request when I visit, the one I have been finessing for decades, and the one that still surprises me regularly by its deliciousness. Some friends (like the teenaged Liam) request my bolognese lasagna with detailed demands, specifying that I make the pasta sheets fresh myself instead of the "cheater's lasagna" (whereby I purchase fresh pasta), and insisting on "no fewer than four layers." If you feel up for a few extra steps, the lasagna, even the cheater's version, is worth it. But the bolognese sauce is the key, and even tossed over some fresh tagliatelle or a box of dried penne, it always satisfies.

A keen observer might note that nowhere within these pages lies a recipe calling for celery. Though not as ubiquitous as the eggplant haters, we who abhor celery are out there, and this book is for us. As seen below, I usually rely on fennel bulb where tradition may have called for celery. It adds so much more to the layering of flavors of the insaporire and has the added benefit of not tasting like celery.

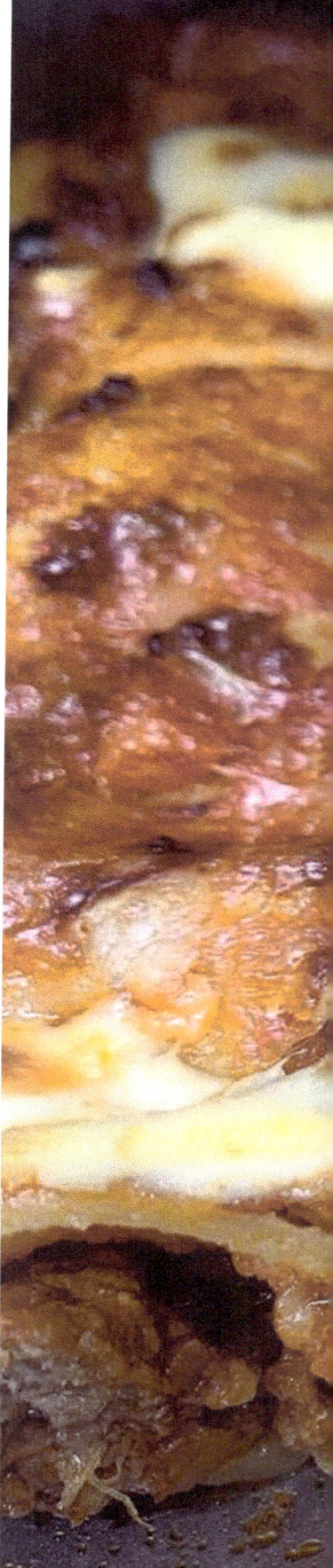

Bolognese lasagna

INGREDIENTS

¼ cup diced bacon, pancetta, prosciutto or guanciale

1 onion, peeled, trimmed and finely diced

1 fennel bulb, trimmed and finely diced

2 carrots, peeled and finely cubed

Olive oil

1 pound ground beef (80/20)

1 pound ground pork

½ cup dry white wine

1 cup whole milk

28 oz can tomato purée

28 oz beef or chicken broth (preferably homemade!)

Salt

Pepper

BÉCHAMEL SAUCE

4 Tbsp butter

4 Tbsp flour

2 cups whole milk

1 garlic clove, peeled

¼ tsp freshly ground nutmeg

1 bay leaf

Salt

Pepper

1 pound lasagna sheets, fresh or oven-ready dried pasta

1 cup grated Parmesan cheese

In a large heavy-bottomed Dutch oven, heat a glug of olive oil over medium heat. Add the cured pork and sauté until browned. Add the diced onions with a pinch of salt and sauté for a few minutes. Add the fennel and continue sautéing. Add the carrots with another pinch of salt and continue to sauté for another few minutes. Add both ground meats and, using a flat bottom sided wooden spoon, stir to break up the meat as it browns. Generously salt and pepper the meat as it cooks.

Once the meat has cooked through, add the white wine and deglaze, scraping the bottom of the pan to incorporate the fond into the liquid. After the wine largely evaporates, add the milk. Lower the heat to medium low so the meat and vegetables simmer rather than boil furiously in the milk. After about five minutes of occasional stirring, add the tomato purée and the broth (swirling the broth in the empty tomato can to get the dregs of the tomato purée).

After everything comes to a boil, lower the heat so the sauce is at a bare simmer. Cover with a slightly askew lid and simmer for 2 hours, stirring every half hour or so. Taste and salt if necessary.

Meanwhile, make the béchamel sauce. In a saucepan, melt the butter. Add the flour and stir together for about 45 seconds. Whisk the milk in slowly. Add the garlic clove, nutmeg, bay leaf, and a pinch of salt and pepper, and cook on low for 5-10 minutes, stirring periodically until the sauce thickens. Remove from heat. Before assembling lasagna, remove bay leaf and garlic.

To assemble, layer in a 7 x 11 or 9 x 13 baking dish, starting with about ¼ cup of bolognese sauce. Then layer: pasta, 1 cup of bolognese sauce, ½ cup béchamel, and ¼ cup Parmesan, salt and pepper. Continue layering in this order for at least 3 more layers, using up all the ingredients.

Bake in a 400°F oven for 10 minutes; raise to 450°F and continue baking for an additional 8 minutes.

Caesar salad

I love Caesar salad. High brow, low brow, I don't care. I'll order it at an airport chain or make the trek to Zuni in San Francisco for the Platonic Ideal of Caesar. (And yes, if anyone argues that a Caesar could never be transformative or life changing, take them to Zuni). And also yes, Caesar salad originated in Mexico City rather than Italy, but it is in this chapter anyway.

Homemade Caesar is among the best Caesars. You can tailor it to your precise preference: I like mine with a heavy hand of anchovy, generous coarsely ground black pepper and loads of freshly grated Parmigiano Reggiano.

INGREDIENTS

2 garlic cloves

1 lemon

2 tsp anchovy paste or 4 anchovy filets

1 tsp Dijon mustard

¼ cup mayonnaise or freshly made aioli

½ tsp freshly ground peppercorn

2 heads little gem lettuces or 1 head romaine

¼ cup Parmesan cheese

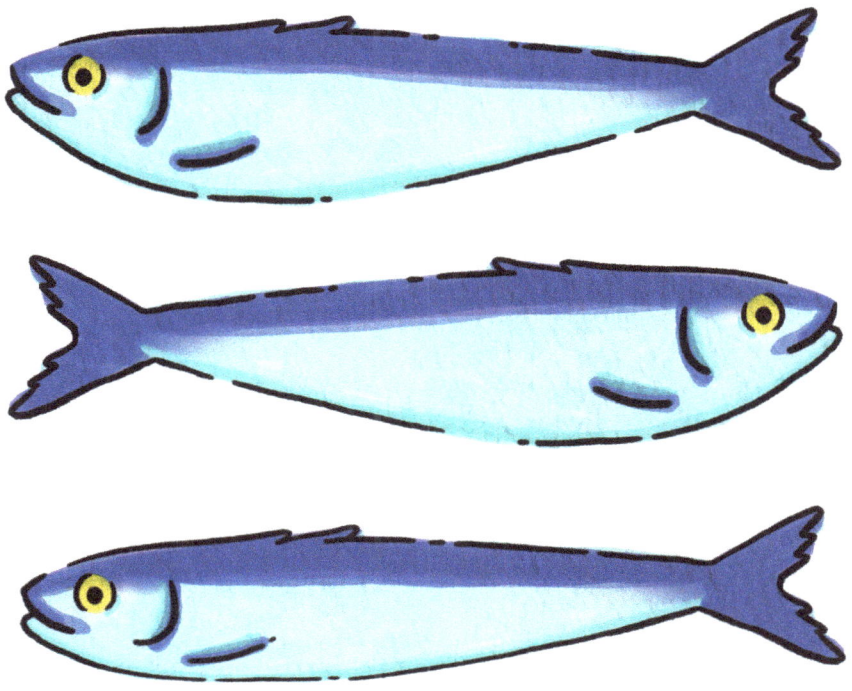

To make the Caesar dressing, pound into a paste 2 garlic cloves, zest from the lemon and a pinch of salt in a mortar and pestle. Add the anchovy paste or filets and pound into the garlic. Add the juice from the lemon and let sit for a few minutes so the acid mellows out the raw garlic. Then add and blend in the Dijon mustard, mayonnaise or aioli and pepper. Taste and add more lemon juice or anchovy if needed.

Clean and dry the lettuce very well. I prefer to use whole leaves but chop if desired. Apply the dressing generously and then top liberally with black pepper and Parmesan.

You can use a food processor instead of mortar and pestle, but the flavors will be more subtle without the pounded extraction of the oils.

Pork braised in milk with sage butter

I first encountered pork braised in milk during my year in Italy and it was love at first taste. The milk and cream transform into a thickened golden sauce adorning a meltingly tender meat. While the result is not the prettiest dish, it is certainly among the most delicious.

When I served this at La Musette, there were customers who jumped at it and others who wearily ordered it at my urging, but both sets would come out to the truck with slightly larger eyes twinkling with cartoon-like stars in them after finishing the plate to sing its praises. The higher fat content in the dairy is key to the textural transformation so do not substitute the whole milk or cream with a skim milk.

This recipe was adapted from a Saveur article originally published sometime between 2000 and 2003. As is the case with most of my favorite dishes, I will usually read a recipe or order something at a restaurant and then continue to cook it, rebuilding it from memory each time so that it slowly evolves through the years.

INGREDIENTS

3 pounds boneless pork chops, roast or shoulder

Olive oil

2 Tbsp butter

30 fresh sage leaves

1 cup whole milk

2 cups half-and-half or heavy cream

Zest of 1 lemon, preferably Meyer

Salt

Salt the pork generously. Combine the olive oil and butter in a Dutch oven and sear the pork on all sides. Transfer the meat to a plate.

Fry 10 fresh sage leaves in the hot oil for 30 seconds and set aside as garnish. Fry 10 more and leave them in the pan. Return the meat and any juices to the pan and slowly pour the milk and cream in until the pork is mostly but not fully submerged. Zest the lemon directly into the pot with a cocktail zest peeler, as pictured on page 34. A microplane zester will not extract the essential oil from the skin like the cocktail zester, but is fine if that's all you have. Add the remaining 10 fresh sage leaves to the liquid.

Simmer gently, partially covered for 1½-3 hours, depending on the size of the meat. Pork chops will take less time and a full roast will take longer. (You can cut a roast into quarters to shorten the braising time.) Turn the meat over halfway through cooking. When done, the meat will be falling apart tender and the liquid will have thickened into a chunky golden sauce.

Slice or fork the pork into chunks and serve with the thickened sauce poured on top and the reserved fried sage leaves strewn about.

Pasta all'arrabbiata

Pasta all'arrabbiata, or "angry" pasta, reminds me of my halcyon days of youth. After returning from a year in Italy and graduating from Wellesley, this was my go-to recipe as I settled into my first adult apartment. It takes about 20 minutes to throw together so I would cook it once a week after a long day at the office. It's a dish that rarely yields leftovers because it is so satisfying and addictive that you finish the pot. Because of its short cook time and high deliciousness ratio, this was also a perfect staff meal at the Wheel House.

Technically, I make what Liam would also call "cheater's arrabbiata." Worry not, this does not entail any torrid affairs; rather, the recipe relies on spicy Italian sausage to do half of the angry lifting. In Boulder, the butchers at Lucky's Market (a local quality shop not to be confused with the large California supermarket chain of yore) make my favorite hot Italian pork sausages.

INGREDIENTS

1 pound penne pasta

1 onion

2 hot Italian pork sausages

2 cloves garlic

1 serrano or other hot pepper

28 oz pureed tomato sauce

Salt

Pepper

Olive oil

Parmesan to grate

Place a large pot of water on to boil while assembling the sauce. Once the water has come to a boil, add 1 tablespoon salt and lower heat to a gentle boil.

Dice the onion and sauté with 1 teaspoon salt in a glug of olive oil over medium heat until translucent, about 5 minutes. Slice the raw sausage lengthwise to remove from the casing and add the meat to the onions. Using a flat-ended wooden spoon, break the sausage meat up into small chunks as you continue to sauté and mix the meat with the onions. While the meat cooks, mince the garlic cloves and deseed and mince the hot pepper. Once the sausage has cooked through, add the minced garlic and hot pepper to the pan. Sauté for an additional 30 seconds and then add the tomato sauce to the pan. Add about half a cup of water to the empty can or jar, swirl around to collect the dregs of the sauce, and pour into the pan. Stir to incorporate and let the sauce simmer as you cook the pasta.

Add the dry pasta to a large pot of generously-salted boiling water. Stir periodically to ensure it doesn't stick together. Taste the sauce as it cooks and add more salt if necessary. When the pasta is done to your liking (al dente or fully cooked), strain, and add to the pan of sauce. Stir vigorously to fully coat the pasta.

Serve in a pasta bowl, topped with freshly grated Parmesan and freshly cracked pepper.

Pasta alla carbonara

When I am too tired to cook, I make carbonara. Bacon and egg pasta always sounds appealing, the ingredients are usually on hand, and it takes only 20 minutes to throw together. Likewise, at La Musette, if folks showed up unexpectedly or if I ran out of everything on the menu and needed an easy staff meal, this was my solution.

Carbonara is a recipe subject to fervent loyalty to regional variations. I learned mine in Florence from my Italian friend Daniela, although I suspect the recipe has mutated somewhere along the hundreds of times I have made it. I adhere vehemently to the proscription against cream or butter, but am more flexible on the form of cured pig and dry cheese.

Timing is important in this recipe. The pork and aromatics must be cooked and piping hot right when the pasta finishes cooking. I start heating the water and make sure everything is minced and ready before putting the pasta in to cook. This affords about 7 minutes to sauté the cured meat and aromatics.

INGREDIENTS

1 pound spaghetti

¼ pound cured pig, cubed or lardooned: guanciale, pancetta or bacon

1 small onion, minced

1 small shallot, minced

2 clove, minced

2 large fresh eggs, at room temperature

⅓ cup freshly grated dry cheese: pecorino, parm, dry jack or a combination thereof

Freshly ground pepper

Salt

Olive oil

Bring a large pot of water to a boil and then add 1-2 tablespoons of salt. Add the pasta, cooking until al dente, and stirring occasionally. When done, reserve 1 cup of the cooking liquid, strain the pasta and immediately return to the hot cooking pot.

Meanwhile, begin cooking the cured pork in a cast iron or heavy-bottomed pan. Stir frequently until browned and crispy. There should be a good amount of pork fat rendered, but if not, add a tablespoon of olive oil. Sauté the minced onion and shallot with a pinch of salt in the hot oil until softened. Add the garlic for the final 30 seconds of sautéing. This should be ready as soon as your pasta finishes cooking. If it is done early, pull off the heat until the pasta is cooked and quickly bring back to piping hot before adding to pasta.

Once the cooked pasta returns to the hot cooking pot (with the burner turned off), crack both eggs into the pasta and start stirring vigorously. Add the grated cheese while continuing to stir. Then add the bacon, onions and hot fat, still stirring vigorously. Add ⅛ cup of cooking liquid and continue stirring. The heat of the ingredients will cook the eggs while the vigorous stirring creates an emulsion and makes the sauce slightly creamy.

Serve in pasta bowls with more grated cheese and ground pepper. Ensure that each serving has a generous topping of the cured meat and other goodies.

WINTERS IN NIWOT

NIWOT COLORADO

CHAPTER 6:
Winters in Niwot

I love Boulder County in part because of its dramatic, yet ultimately temperate climate. The Rockies meet the High Plains and the skies dazzle with intense weather patterns. We might see picturesque snowstorms, whirring cloud formations, northern lights, schizophrenic electrical storms, violent hailstorms, or a week of permafrost... and yet it is always followed by a spate of mild, reasonable weather. The snow melts, the clouds dissipate, the thunder recesses, and everyone returns to their outdoor nature excursions. So in Niwot, folks are bundled up at home, watching the heavy snow from the security of their cozy homes until the weather breaks and then they flock to the bar and the streets, starved for a dose of human interaction.

And Niwot, of course, is happy to provide a number of events for the community to come out seeking said human interactions. Après Ski and Wine About Winter are two of the town-wide days luring locals to stroll around Niwot, shop and share a glass of wine or a warm beverage designed to brighten the short dark days with community.

I had a love/hate relationship with winters in Niwot. The iced over sidewalk in front of the food truck was a constant peril as I scurried back and forth between the bar (my commissary kitchen) and the food truck with once-piping-hot fare for customers inside. Being a Californian and working over a blazing stove, I of course never dressed properly for the snow or the ice. (A regular even once gifted me his old puffy down jacket, observing that I didn't seem to have a proper winter coat, and even now, every time I put it on, I'm still amazed at how it actually keeps the cold out!) But also, I love winter cooking.

Winter food is so cozy and comforting. It warms the body and warms the heart. Intensifying the flavors from a long braise or stew brings new dimensions to the food unavailable to the quicker cooking summer techniques. I believe that the food we eat should be shaped by the seasons, both in terms of the ingredients available, and what the colder temperatures mean for cooking and cravings.

Butternut squash soup

Butternut squash soup was a staple of La Musette's winter and fall repertoires. It is among the quickest and easiest recipes in the book and if it were in a hiking guide, it would be a "1 boot" for easiness and "9 mountain" for beauty pay off — a great ratio!

Its versatility accommodates many dietary restrictions. It can be prepared vegan or with an increased richness from chicken broth and cream. Winter squash are local and abundant, store well, and are affordable. A pantry stocked with butternut, delicata, and kabocha squash can salvage those hungry evenings when shopping or eating take-out are unappealing options.

INGREDIENTS

1 large onion, peeled and diced

1 leek, dark green parts removed, cleaned well, diced

1 carrot, peeled and sliced

2 cloves garlic, peeled and minced

1 large butternut squash

6 cups water or chicken broth

1 bay leaf

Salt

Olive oil

¼ cup heavy cream, optional

Peel and deseed the butternut squash. Cut into large chunks, douse with olive oil and salt and roast for 20 minutes at 400°F. This step can be omitted, but roasting draws out the squash's flavors better than simmering does.

Meanwhile, heat 2 tablespoons of olive oil in a large heavy-bottomed pot. Sauté the onion with a pinch of salt until translucent. Add the leek and sauté for a few minutes. Then add the carrot and sauté for a few minutes. Add the minced garlic and sauté for 30 seconds. Add the squash, a bay leaf and 6 cups of liquid. Scrape the bottom of the pan after adding the liquid to incorporate any fond from the sautéed vegetables into the soup.

Bring to a boil and let simmer for 20 minutes (or longer if the squash was not pre-roasted.) The squash should be easily pierce-able with a fork when ready. Blend with an immersion blender in the pot, or pour into a blender in batches to purée. Adjust salt if necessary. Add the cream if using, or an additional drizzle of olive oil for the vegan version. Bring back to just under a boil to serve.

Garnish if desired with a dollop of sour cream or pesto, a swirl of olive oil, freshly ground pepper or some toasted pumpkin seeds.

Pot roast

Winter is the time for food that comforts and warms our souls. When you are looking out at another beautiful snowfall, you want food that feels like a cozy blanket wrapped around your shoulders, feet tucked under you, your favorite book waiting on your lap for your attention to return from the storm outside, the sound of the fireplace crackling on the periphery of your senses. Pot roast is the dish that evokes those feelings, even if the idyllic scene is only in your head.

My grandmothers, particularly the Ohio contingent, made pot roasts regularly but it seems to be a dish that has fallen out of rotation with later generations. The preparation is relatively quick and simple, but it is followed by hours of cooking, so perhaps the increased ability to work from home will spark a pot roast renaissance. If you can take a 15-minute break to throw the dish together and put it in the oven, you can return to work and have virtually no food prep when dinnertime rolls around.

INGREDIENTS

3 pounds beef roast like brisket or chuck

2 onions

2 cloves garlic

4 carrots

4-6 potatoes, preferable Yukon gold or another waxy variety

1 bay leaf

1 Tbsp dijon mustard

½ cup red wine

32 oz beef or chicken stock (Better Than Bouillon works well) or water

Olive oil

Salt

Pepper

Preheat the oven to 350°F. Cut the beef into a few large chunks and generously salt and pepper them. Heat up a Dutch oven, or similar cooking vessel. Add a glug of olive oil and add the meat, searing on high heat for about 6 minutes, turning periodically so all sides brown.

While searing the meat, peel and cut up the rest of the vegetables. Cut the onions into wedges and add to the meat once it is browned. Gently smash the garlic and toss in as whole cloves. After peeling the carrots, cut them in thirds and add them to the pot. Cut the potato into quarters and add to the pot.* Add the dijon mustard and the red wine. After the wine hits the hot pot, scrape the fond — the browned caked-on bits from the meat and vegetables adhering to the bottom of the pan — vigorously so the flavor morsels incorporate into the liquid. Then add the stock and a bay leaf. Beef broth will make the richest and most flavorful pot roast and water the least so, but this recipe is very forgiving so use what is available.

Bring to a boil and then cover tightly with foil and the dutch oven lid. Put the pot in the oven and let cook at 350°F for at least 90 minutes. After 90 minutes, use a fork or knife to test how tender the meat is. Let cook for another half hour if needed to soften the meat.

Serve in a shallow pasta bowl or raised edge plate with the meat and vegetables nestled in a small amount of the

* If you prefer your carrots and potatoes to be less soft and mushy, you can wait until the last 45 minutes of cooking to add them to the pot.

Shepherd's pie

This is not an old family recipe, nor is it technically even a shepherd's pie. Folks in Niwot kept asking for shepherd's pie so I put one together for the food truck. With ground beef instead of lamb, this is a cottage pie rather than shepherd's, but apparently the shepherds had better PR agents than those living in cottages.

My recipe is a straight-forward, no-frills version. It is a quick and easy dinner, even more so if you have mashed potatoes left over from last night's dinner. This is Niwot comfort food, and is especially satisfying on a snowy night when you do not want to leave the house.

INGREDIENTS

4 large russet potatoes

1 stick of butter

¼ cup whole milk

1 pound ground beef

1 onion, trimmed and diced

2 carrots, peeled and diced

1 leek, trimmed and diced
(optional)

1 cup frozen peas

1 Tbsp flour (optional: omit to make gluten free)

2 cups chicken or beef broth

Salt

Pepper

Olive oil

Peel and cut the potatoes into large chunks. Boil the potatoes in a large pot of salted water until very soft, drain, and return to the pot. Add ½-1 stick of butter, 2 teaspoons salt and half of the milk. Replace the lid and let sit for a couple of minutes so the butter will melt. Mash with a potato masher until smooth. Taste and add more salt to taste. Add more milk or butter if necessary for a creamy texture and to taste. Set aside.

Heat a sauté pan over medium heat and add a glug of olive oil. Add the ground meat and break it up as it cooks with a flat-bottomed wooden spoon. Salt and pepper the meat as it cooks, adding about ½ teaspoon salt and ⅛ teaspoon pepper. Once the meat has browned, add the onions and another pinch of salt. Sauté, stirring periodically, for a few minutes until the onions have turned translucent. Add the leeks and continue sautéing. There should be sufficient oil with the rendered fat from the meat, but if the pan looks dry, add more olive oil to prevent the vegetables from burning as they sauté. After a few minutes, add the carrots and cook for a few additional minutes. Sprinkle the flour into the fat in the pan and stir until it forms a paste. Add the frozen peas and broth. Stir, scraping any fond from the bottom of the pan into the mixture and mixing any flour clumps into the broth. Let simmer for a few minutes and then taste for seasoning, adding more salt or pepper as needed.

Pour the meat and vegetable mixture into a baking dish, including the thickened liquid, but make sure the liquid does not cover the mixture entirely. The mashed potatoes should sit atop the meat and vegetables rather than float on gravy. Spoon the mashed potatoes on top and spread with a plastic spatula so the surface is smooth and fully covers all of the meat and vegetables.

Bake at 350°F for 20 minutes until the potatoes have a golden brown crust.

Quiche Lorraine

I don't know who this Lorraine was, but boy, did she have expensive taste in quiche ingredients! At least in my adaptation, this recipe is neither quick and easy, nor cost effective. But it is delicious and a slice of quiche with a vinegary green salad is a perfect lunch or brunch offering for guests you actually like. It is also convenient to prepare ahead and serve quickly when there is a mob of people roaming the streets of Niwot and needing fuel for their community event activities.

It is always worth making the pie dough from scratch, but I'll never know if you buy a pre-made crust (unless I'm the lunch guest!) I prefer Paris ham or Framanni smoked ham, but in any case, find a hunk of ham rather than thinly sliced deli meat so you can have the right sized cubes.

PIE CRUST

1½ cups flour

½ tsp salt

½ cup (1 stick) butter

1 cup ice water mixed with 2 Tbsp apple cider vinegar

FILLING

3 slices thick bacon, cut into lardons

1 large yellow onion

1 cup Paris ham, cut into ½ inch cubes

1 cup Gruyére cheese, cut into ½ inch cubes

⅓ cup Parmesan, freshly grated on large holes of a grater

6 eggs

1 cup cream

Salt

Pepper

Preheat the oven to 400°F. Crack the eggs into a bowl and whisk them together with the cream. Let the mixture rest in the fridge while preparing the rest of the recipe. To achieve a creamy texture of quiche, the eggs need to settle and lose the aeration from whisking.

Make the pie dough in a large bowl or food processor. Add half of the butter to the flour and salt and mix by hand or machine until the texture is a mealy flour. Add the second half of butter and pulse briefly or use a pastry cutter so the butter is left in larger pea-sized chunks. Drizzle 6-7 tablespoons of the vinegary ice water over the dough, and bring it together with as little mixing as possible. When the dough comes together, make a thick flat disc and wrap tightly in plastic wrap. Refrigerate while assembling the rest of the ingredients.

The two different textures of butter in the dough from the two additions make for a particularly flaky crust.

Quiche Lorraine

Cook the lardons of bacon in a cast iron pan, stirring periodically. Meanwhile, peel the onion and cut into slices from root end to stem end, latitudinally. When the bacon has just turned crispy, add the onions and 1 teaspoon of salt. Sauté the onions in the bacon fat with the bacon bits still in the pan until the onions turn golden and translucent. Remove from heat.

Remove the dough from the fridge and roll out into a large circle, about ⅛ inch thick. I use the plastic that the dough was wrapped in on the bottom and another piece of plastic on top of the dough so it doesn't stick to the surface or the rolling pin (a clean empty wine bottle works as a rolling pin if it is a Sky Zinfandel claret style bottle with flat sides). After rolling out, use the plastic wrap to transfer the dough to the pie pan.

Use a deep-sided 10 inch pie dish or springform pan so the crust will accommodate all of the filling. Make a nice edge of the pie crust by pinching the dough between the thumb and two next fingers. Prick the dough with a fork several times, line with parchment paper and weigh down with dry beans (this will help the crust maintain its shape and not shrink). Prebake the pie crust for 10 minutes at 400°F.

Remove the crust from the oven, discard the parchment and dry beans, and lower the oven to 375°F. Let the crust cool slightly. Layer the onions and bacon atop the pie crust. Strew the cubes of ham and gruyere evenly over the onions. Gently pour the egg and cream mixture over the ham and cheese, ensuring it fills the pie shell up to the base of the pinched edge. Sprinkle the grated Parmesan on top and season with freshly ground pepper and a pinch of salt.

Bake at 375°F for 45 minutes. Check to see if the quiche is set by gently shaking the pan to see if the eggs are still jiggly. If so, bake for an additional 5-10 minutes to allow the eggy mixture to fully set. The quiche should be golden brown. Cover lightly with foil if it is getting too dark.

Serve hot or cold, with a simple green salad.

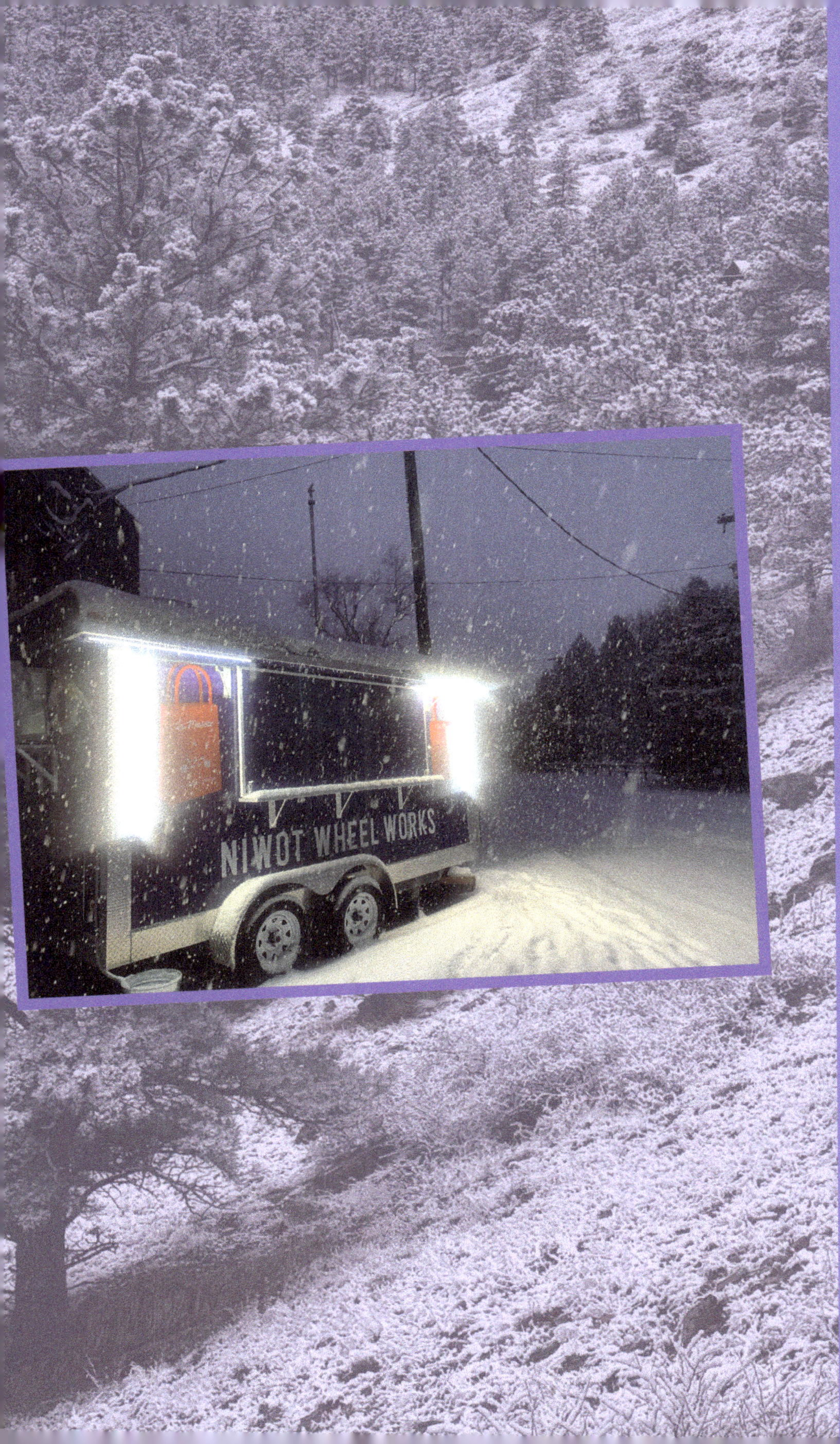

6. WINTERS IN NIWOT | QUICHE LORRAINE

Vichyssoise potato leek soup

Massillon, Ohio is home to the famed Massillon Tigers, a high school football team that embodies the Friday Night Lights narrative. My stepmom Linn grew up there and I have fond childhood memories visiting the Ohio grandparents. I learned many of my favorite comfort food recipes from Linn and Grandma Briner.

Grandpa Briner was the local small town pharmacist and president of the Tigers Boosters club. The football game I attended with him was unforgettable and a much-relayed story when fielding questions at La Musette about why I had so many Massillon Tiger tee shirts. I learned that there's a surprising number of Ohio transplants in the Niwot community.

This potato leek soup is one of those Briner family recipes I grew up with. It is fairly quick and easy to prepare, can easily be made vegetarian or vegan, and brings a soul-satisfying deliciousness that far exceeds its relatively humble list of ingredients.

INGREDIENTS

Olive oil

2 large leeks (4 or 5 if you have smaller spring leeks)

3 large Yukon gold potatoes

1 bay leaf

2 quarts chicken broth (preferably homemade, but packaged or Better Than Bouillon works), vegetable broth, or water

Salt

Pepper

Optional: ¼ cup cream

To properly clean the leeks, which often have significant dirt hidden between the layers, trim the stringy roots off the bottom, trim half an inch off of the dark tops, and then slice in half lengthwise all the way down the leek. Soak both halves in plenty of cold water for a few minutes, periodically shaking the leeks and physically separating the layers to remove any visible dirt. The dirt usually collects in the light yellowy-green layers halfway up the stalk. Remove from water and slice the leeks from the white bottom to the very green top into ¼ inch thick half moons.

In a large heavy-bottomed pot over medium heat, add a generous glug of olive oil and sauté the leeks with 1 teaspoon of kosher salt with a flat bottomed wooden spoon. Meanwhile, rinse the potatoes and cut into halves, and then ¼ inch slices. Once the leeks take on a translucent shine, add the potatoes and keep stirring periodically. Add another glug of olive oil. Season with another teaspoon of salt, ½ teaspoon of freshly ground pepper, and a bay leaf.

After a few minutes of sautéing, pour the stock or water over the leeks and potatoes, covering with at least 2 extra inches of liquid. Scrape the fond off the bottom of the pan to incorporate any caramelized bits.

Simmer for 20-30 minutes until the potatoes can be easily pierced. Remove from heat and if using, add the cream. Blend with an immersion blender or upright blender until smooth. Add more salt and pepper to taste and serve.

Alternatively, leave the soup unblended and add in flour dumplings:

> Mix 1 cup flour, 1 teaspoon salt, and a shy cup of milk or water together until smooth. Drop spoonful size dollops of batter into a pot of salted boiling water. Once they rise to the top, after a couple minutes of cooking, scoop them out with a slotted spoon or strainer. Add dumplings to the hot soup and serve.

SHAPED BY CALIFORNIA'S MEXICAN FOOD

Carnitas

Linn's chile rellenos
with sautéed corn

Gail's posole

Estelli's chicken quesadillas
in tomatillo sauce

Cumin coleslaw

Chicken sopes

Confited duck tostada with
cumin slaw

Green salad with avocados
and cotija cheese in coriander
lime dressing

Halibut ceviche in lettuce cups

CHAPTER 7:
Shaped by California's Mexican Food

The California wine industry is completely dependent upon the skilled labor of its immigrant population and largely fed by the rich culinary traditions of immigrant communities. Since I was young and still today, some of the best food in Sonoma comes from Mexican restaurants and food trucks. Our family traditions and diets were likewise informed by the influence of these communities. We gathered around to make tamales for holidays, cooked carnitas and tacos to feed the masses during harvest meals, and ate quesadillas several nights a week. It was natural for me to incorporate this comfort food into the food truck rotations.

Some of my earliest memories of travel were from camping trips my family took in Mexico when I was quite young. Later trips as an adult were usually food-centered. I stayed by myself for a couple weeks in the small town of La Manzanilla, Jalisco to do an intensive Spanish immersion program. Every day I walked to the local tortilleria and bought corn tortillas so fresh that they were still warm. They were so addictively aromatic and delicious and unlike any tortilla I had had previously or since, that I would polish off half of them on the walk home. I met a woman at the market selling unique tamales who invited me into her home and taught me her family recipes. Although I was there to learn Spanish and recover from heartbreak, the flavors and textures and aromas of La Manzanilla are what left the most significant impact from the trip.

Carnitas

Carnitas are often one of the most delicious elements to many Mexican dishes and relatively easy to make, but often are lackluster when you order it out. The final frying is key to perfect carnitas. Once the meat is cooked, you can make tacos, nachos, burritos, salads or serve it with sides. It is a great dish for a large party, or will last for several meals, especially when stored in its rendered pork fat.

INGREDIENTS

1 boneless pork shoulder or butt (about 5 pounds)

2 cups lard

1 orange

1 bay leaf

Salt

Limes

Cut the pork into large chunks, about the size of a fist, and salt each piece well. You can let it sit overnight salted or use immediately.

In a heavy bottomed pan, melt the lard. Add the meat and the bay leaf. Cut an orange in half, squeeze the juice over the meat and then add the 2 rinds to the pan. The fat and juice should cover partway up the meat. Add water if necessary so the meat is at least ½-¾ submerged. Partially cover and cook on low heat at a very gentle simmer for 3-5 hours, stirring occasionally. The fat from the roast will render additional lard and add to the liquid in the pot as the water and juice evaporate.

Once the meat is meltingly tender, shred the large chunks with two forks. When ready to eat, scoop about 2 tablespoons of lard into a cast iron pan and add up to a cup of the shredded meat. Sear for a few minutes on medium high heat, stirring periodically, until the meat has some crispy edges. Taste for salt and serve with a squeeze of fresh lime. Store leftovers in the fat and crisp up in the cast iron as needed.

Linn's chile rellenos with sautéed corn

My stepmom Linn made the most amazing chili rellenos when I was young. They were fluffy and light with perfectly melty Vella cheese, freshly roasted poblanos, and eggs from our chickens. She cooked 6 or 8 at a time on our double sized cast iron griddle and we ate them immediately before the eggs fell.

This recipe was inspired by my memory of Linn's rellenos and adapted to be easier to make to order in the food truck. I loaded the relleno with seasonal produce and it became a star vegetarian entrée. For variety, sauté whatever combination of vegetables you desire and serve with a fresh salsa or dollop of sour cream, accompanied by a salad or rice and beans.

INGREDIENTS

4 fresh whole poblano peppers

1 small onion

2 Tokyo/Hakurei turnips, peeled and diced

8 green beans, trimmed and diced

2 ears of corn, kernels cut off the cob

1 clove garlic, minced

Olive oil

3 eggs

4 slices melty cheese like Vella Toma or Monterey jack

Grapeseed oil

Fresh basil or cilantro, chopped, for garnish

Roast and blacken the poblanos, using the method described on page 159. After peeling and deseeding, you should have 4 flat triangular pieces.

Sauté the vegetables in a glug of olive oil over medium heat, starting with the onion and a generous pinch of salt, stirring regularly. Once the onion becomes translucent, add each successive vegetable and sauté for a minute or two before adding the next. Once the vegetables are cooked, set aside.

Separate the eggs and place the whites in a large bowl to whisk into soft peaks (use a stand mixer or electric whisk if desired). Add the yolks and a pinch of salt and gently fold into the whites.

Heat a griddle, large cast iron, or nonstick pan and coat with grapeseed oil. With a serving spoon, place generous plops of the egg mixture on the hot pan (as many as comfortably fit in your pan, likely two at a time). Place a poblano pepper on the egg, covering half of the surface of the egg. Layer the cheese and a generous mound of the sautéed vegetables on the poblano. Cover the pan and let cook on medium heat for a few minutes. When the egg is cooked, with a golden brown crust on the bottom, fold the half or third that does not have the poblano and toppings on it over the rest so the egg looks like a taco shell.

Plate, sprinkle with Maldon salt and garnish with fresh herbs.

Gail's posole

This recipe is adapted from Tammy and Cliff Gentry's mother. Tammy was one of the owners of the Wheel House and her brother Cliff booked the live music for the first year or so that La Musette operated. They both warmly welcomed me into the fold and have remained good friends. Tammy and Cliff grew up in New Mexico with an affinity for the Southwestern cuisine their mother Gail cooked. Gail visited them in Niwot regularly and I was fortunate to get to know her through those visits. After she passed away, Tammy shared Gail's posole recipe with me and I featured it on the La Musette menu periodically in her honor. Posole is the Southwestern version of Mexican pozole, a meat stew made with hominy (dried nixtamalized corn kernels) and served with heaps of fresh and flavorful garnishes.

INGREDIENTS

1 whole chicken

3 hot dried peppers

2 onion

1 pound dried hominy, rinsed and soaked in water overnight or 1 large can of cooked hominy

2 stalks green garlic or 3 garlic cloves, minced

Fresh oregano

3 dried ancho and/or Santa Fe chili pods, rinsed, deseeded and crumbled

1 Tbsp powdered shallots or dried onions

1 tsp dried oregano

1 bay leaf

1 tsp powdered cumin

Olive oil

GARNISHES

Radish, thinly sliced

Cilantro, roughly chopped

Jalapeños, sliced

Fresh oregano, chiffonaded

Onion, finely minced

Avocados, cubed

Sour cream

If using dried hominy, cook in plenty of water for 3-4 hours, until it is soft enough to eat. If using canned hominy, skip this step.

Simmer the whole chicken in a large pot of water with 2 tablespoons salt, hot dried peppers and one onion, halved, for 1-2 hours until a rich chicken stock has developed. Remove the chicken and then strain the broth and discard the solids. Pick through the meat, discarding bones and skin and collecting the shredded meat in a bowl for later.

Sauté 1 diced onion in 2 tablespoons olive oil and 1 teaspoon salt over medium heat until translucent. Add minced garlic, 2 tablespoons chiffonaded fresh oregano, crumbled chilis and the rest of the dried herbs. Stir for a minute, and then add the chicken stock, the shredded chicken and the hominy. Simmer for 30 minutes-1 hour. Adjust salt as needed.

Serve piping hot with a heaping pile of all or some of the garnish.

Estellí's chicken quesadillas in tomatillo sauce

Fernando, master mechanic of Niwot Wheel Works, is one of the most generous and competent individuals I've encountered. He fixed countless kitchen gadgets and food truck problems, commiserated when needed, showed up with tequila also when needed, and was one of the most reliable taste testers, especially for anything freshly baked. Plus, he is an absolute delight.

Among the solutions he provided over the years to various La Musette crises was convincing his niece Estellí to visit for a summer and assist in the food truck when I was short-staffed. Like her uncle, Estellí was a delight and tremendously helpful in the food truck. This chicken braised in tomatillo verde sauce is based on her recipe and turned into one of those dishes that continued to be requested for months after it appeared on the menu.

INGREDIENTS

2 pounds tomatillos

3 jalapeños

2 shallots

5 cloves garlic

1 tsp sugar

¼ cup fresh cilantro leaves and stems (the cilantro averse may omit)

8 chicken thighs, deboned and deskinned

1 onion, peeled and sliced longitudinally

Flour tortillas (or corn to make gluten-free)

1 cup freshly grated Monterey jack cheese

Olive oil

Salt

Rinse the tomatillos, jalapeños, shallots and garlic. Toss with olive oil and salt and roast in a 400°F oven on a baking sheet for 20 minutes. Let cool enough to handle, and then deseed the jalapeños, peel the rest of the roasted vegetables, and toss all of it into a blender. Add cilantro if using. Blend until smooth. Taste, and add more salt and 1 teaspoon sugar, if necessary. Pour into a heavy-bottomed pan.

Salt the chicken thighs and submerge in the tomatillo sauce. Cook, covered tightly, in the oven at 350°F or on the stovetop at a simmer until the chicken is tender, about 40 minutes. When done, remove the chicken from the tomatillo sauce and, when cool enough to handle, shred the chicken with fingers or forks. Add 2 cups of the tomatillo sauce back over the shredded chicken. Use the remainder of the sauce for other purposes.

To assemble the quesadillas, heat a cast iron pan over medium heat. Oil the pan with olive oil. Place one tortilla on the warmed pan and cover with a generous amount of grated cheese. Layer ½ cup of the chicken and tomatillo sauce over the cheese and cover with another tortilla. After a few minutes, flip the quesadilla with a large metal spatula. Both sides of the quesadilla should be slightly browned and the cheese melted, but do not overcook or the tortilla will become dry and flaky. Cook quesadillas one at a time.

Cumin coleslaw

Cabbage is an underrated vegetable. It is a heavy lifter in Eastern European cooking and featured prominently during La Musette's Wiglia Polish holiday dinner. I featured my friend Pickle's Surprisingly Delicious Goose Fixins braised cabbage as often as I could at the truck (and handed out the recipe upon repeated requests, since it is actually surprisingly good). I love cabbage in Japanese fare, whether in a soup, or dumplings, or served as an appetizer with a dipping sauce. I once had a braised cabbage with blue cheese and walnut salad at LaLous, a now-closed natural wine bar in Brooklyn that shocked my senses. But usually I rely on a good slaw to incorporate cabbage into a range of dinners.

For me, the fundamentals of a good coleslaw are: garlic, salt, sugar, and vinegar. The Massillon, Ohio-based Briner side of my family are serious about their coleslaw. Theirs is a mayo-based version, not overly sweet and still with a good amount of vinegar, but the real competition in the family comes over how thinly one can slice the cabbage. The recipe below has no mayonnaise but incorporates lessons from the Briners and a nice balance of the other fundamentals. This recipe was initially inspired by a slaw in Big Small Plates, a cookbook from Cindy Pawlcyn, one of the great Napa chefs and restaurateurs.

INGREDIENTS

2 cloves garlic, minced

1 Tbsp sugar

1 tsp salt

1 Tbsp toasted cumin seeds

1 jalapeño pepper, deseeded and minced

1 head cabbage

2 carrots, peeled

1 bunch small radish, cleaned and trimmed

¼ cup champagne or brown rice vinegar

Juice of 1 lime

½ bunch cilantro leaves, cleaned and trimmed off the big stems

Olive oil, optional

In a salad bowl, macerate the minced garlic in the salt and sugar for a few minutes to mellow the sharpness. Squeeze the lime onto the garlic and add the cumin seeds and minced pepper. Pour in the vinegar and stir well to dissolve the sugar into the liquid. Let the dressing rest while preparing the vegetables.

Cut the cabbage into quarters and remove the dense stalk section. Slice the cabbage as thinly as possible, either with a sharp knife and patience, or with a mandoline and utmost caution. As my good friend Caroline notes, perhaps forgo the mandoline if you are already a couple margaritas in. Thinly slice the carrots and radish, ideally with the mandoline, paper thin. Toss all the vegetables in the vinegary dressing. Taste and add salt as needed, up to an additional teaspoon or more. If you prefer a less vinegary salad, add a few tablespoons of olive oil and toss well.

Serve with a mound of cilantro on the coleslaw.

Chicken sopes

Sopes are a Mexican street food made of thick masa cakes with various toppings. The thickness is similar to an arepa or pupusa but ingredients are mounded atop the masa cake taco-style rather than stuffed inside. My recipe below is less traditional in that it mixed some of the toppings into the masa cakes, but evolved into this during a flurry of production while cooking against a deadline for a large party.

I liked to make sopes for large private events and La Musette catering gigs. They can quickly be made in large batches, are easy to eat by hand while milling around at a cocktail party, are a great vehicle for a variety of toppings, and retain their integrity when sitting out on a platter for a while. So whip up a batch for your next party!

INGREDIENTS

1 whole chicken

2 onions, peeled and sliced latitudinally

3 cups masa harina corn flour

1½ cups chicken broth or water

1 can refried beans, or 1 cup dried beans, soaked and cooked

Avocados, perfectly ripe

Sriracha

¼ cup sour cream

Salt

Olive oil

Grapeseed oil

Preheat the oven to 400°F. Place a large cast iron pan in the oven while preheating.

In a large metal bowl, toss the whole chicken and the sliced onions with 2 tablespoons of olive oil and 2 teaspoons of salt. Once the oven is ready, remove the cast iron pan with an oven mitt and transfer the onions and chicken to the pan, with the chicken sitting atop a bed of onions. Roast for 50-60 minutes. (This is my basic roasted chicken recipe, although I add carrots and potatoes to the bed of onions if I'm having it as a stand alone meal.)

Remove the pan from the oven and transfer the chicken to a plate, pouring any liquid from its cavity back into the pan. Measure the masa harina in a large bowl and pour the onions and all of the pan juices into the masa harina, scraping the pan to get any tasty flavor bits stuck to the bottom. If the chicken has released any additional drippings onto its plate, pour those in as well. Add 1½ cups chicken broth or water to the masa harina and stir with a wooden spoon to fully incorporate. Knead the masa for a few minutes and cover with a damp clean kitchen towel until you are ready to cook.

Prepare your toppings before frying up the sopes: heat the refried beans; remove the chicken meat from the carcass and shred, salting if necessary and reserving the chicken skin separately; cube and salt the avocados; mix the sriracha and sour cream together until smooth. If using dried beans instead of canned, after soaking overnight, cook with ample water and 2 teaspoons of salt. When cooked through, transfer beans and 1 cup of the cooking liquid to a blender (add 1 teaspoon powdered shallots or garlic if desired) and blend into a thick but pourable consistency, adding more cooking liquid as needed.

When ready for the final step, take a golf ball sized chunk of the masa, shape into a sphere and flatten with your palms, a tortilla press, or between parchment paper under a heavy pan. The masa cake should be about 3 inches in diameter and ½-inch thick. Prepare 3 to cook and then shape the next batch as you cook up the first.

Over medium heat in a cast iron pan with a thin layer of hot grapeseed oil, fry 3 masa cakes at a time (or however many comfortably fit in the pan), flipping once golden brown and crispy on each side. Transfer to a warm platter once cooked and fry up another batch, adding more grapeseed oil between batches as necessary. There will be at least 12 masa cakes.

Cut the reserved chicken skin into 2-inch rough squares and fry up in the remaining grapeseed oil until crispy, flipping once.

Layer toppings on the warm masa cakes: beans, shredded chicken, avocados and sriracha crema. Garnish with a few leaves of cilantro and top with a fried chicken skin, tilted like a graduation cap.

Confited duck tostada with cumin slaw

The recipe below is quick and easy, as long as you have recently made duck confit (page 53), cumin coleslaw (page 127) and pickled vegetables with onions (page 79). Which is to say, this is a perfect dish to make when you have leftovers. I am not a fan of leftovers. Generally, I will not eat the same meal more than one time in a row. So when I make too much, I either aggressively foist it on guests to take home, or I transform it into a new dish. The crispy tostada is an ideal new dish since it comes together quickly, will taste dramatically different from the preceding meal and is flexible enough to accommodate all variety of repurposed meats and side dishes.

INGREDIENTS

- 4 small 4- or 6-inch flour tortillas (or use corn to make gluten-free)
- 2 duck confit legs
- 1 cup cumin coleslaw
- Pickled onions
- ½ cup sour cream
- 2 Tbsp sriracha
- Duck fat or grapeseed oil
- 8 sprigs cilantro

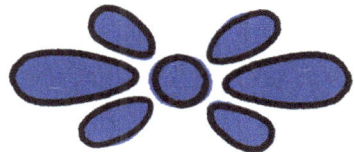

Remove the skin from the duck legs and set aside whole. Remove the meat from the duck legs, shredding it apart with fingers or forks.

Mix the sour cream and sriracha until smooth.

In a large cast iron pan, heat enough duck fat or grapeseed oil to cover the bottom surface with about ¼ inch of oil. Place the duck skin in the hot oil, face down, and let crisp up. Flip halfway through to ensure both sides are crispy. Remove from heat and crumble when cool enough to handle.

Fry the tortillas in the hot oil, one at a time. The tortilla should brown and crisp within 10-40 seconds. If not fully submerged in oil, flip and brown the other side. After cooking all the tortillas, pour off some of the oil, leaving only enough that the cast iron looks greasy. Toss the duck meat in and crisp it up, stirring occasionally, for a couple minutes.

Place a tortilla on each plate. Spread a thin layer of sriracha cream on each tortilla. Evenly distribute the duck meat, the coleslaw, the pickled onions, and the crumbled crispy duck skin on each tortilla. Top with cilantro and serve.

Green salad with avocados and cotija cheese in coriander lime dressing

A year or two after the fires, I moved to New York to search for a new place in the world. I ended up working in the Hamptons for the summer at Carissa's, a trendy bar and restaurant being opened by some friends as an extension to the fabulous pre-existing bakery. This was my only official kitchen restaurant experience prior to running La Musette. The frenetic summer was exhausting and exhilarating, full of both myth-proving and myth-shattering experiences of restaurant work, life in the Hamptons as "the help," new friendships, and, of course, heightened culinary senses, lessons, and experimentation.

This coriander lime dressing is inspired by one of the salads our Head Chef Molly Levine put on the opening menu. Salad dressing can either be the focal point or a background player in a salad, and this one shines as it leads with bold flavors. At La Musette, I ended up pairing it often with my Mexican fare, as the bright coriander and lime danced well with the flavor profile of cumin, cilantro and chilis woven into many of the other dishes.

INGREDIENTS

Mixed lettuces, washed and dried thoroughly

1 ripe avocado

¼ cup toasted pepitas

⅛ cup crumbled cotija cheese (or substitute feta or goat cheese)

DRESSING

1 tsp whole coriander seeds

1 tsp honey

2 limes

4 Tbsp olive oil

Salt

Place the whole coriander seeds in a mortar and pestle with a pinch of salt. Zest one of the limes into the mortar and pestle, using the cocktail zester pictured on page 34 so the oils from the zest are included in the dressing. Pound the seeds and zest together until mixed well. All of the coriander seeds should be broken apart, but a chunky texture is fine. Juice the limes into the mortar (there should be about 2 ounces of lime juice). Move the mixture to a blender, scraping clean the mortar with a plastic spatula. Add the honey and olive oil and blend until the dressing has emulsified.

Assemble the salad, reserving half of the cheese and pepitas to add after dressing. Dress just before serving by tossing with 2-3 tablespoons of dressing. Taste to determine if you need additional dressing. No one likes a soggy salad so it is important not to over-dress. Start with less than needed and incrementally add more after tossing well. After appropriately dressed, make sure to scoop up the goodies from the bottom of the bowl and strew back over the top of the lettuces, along with the remaining reserved pepitas and cheese so the salad presents nicely.

If the limes failed to yield an ounce each, add enough vinegar to fill.

Halibut ceviche in lettuce cups

Halibut ceviche is another dish I associate with my summer in the kitchen in the Hamptons. I loved cooking staff meals at Carissa's and this dish was something I prepared for staff when we had an excess of fresh fluke (a nice white fish) on hand. It was a hit and ended up being my first creation to make it to the official menu. The key to this recipe is a delicateness created by the particular care in preparing the relatively simple ingredients, finely and uniformly minced. The addition of the oil-dense avocado balances the acidity of the lime juice used to "cook" the fish.

Ceviche is often served on or with tortilla chips, but I like the freshness of the little gem lettuces as the vehicle for the ceviche, as did many of the health-conscious Niwotians who embraced this dish.

INGREDIENTS

½ pound fresh halibut

1 large shallot

2 cloves garlic

1-2 Thai bird chilis, deseeded

2 limes

1 large perfectly ripe avocado

4 small radishes

1-2 heads little gem lettuces/ baby romaine or other crisp small lettuce

Cilantro

Salt

Trim and finely dice the halibut into ½-inch cubes. Mince the shallot, garlic, and chilis as finely and uniformly as possible, and add to the fish. Salt the fish and aromatics and gently toss. Clean the limes and zest one of them over the fish. Squeeze the juice from both limes onto the fish.

Return the seasoned fish to the fridge, tossing periodically so the lime juice thoroughly coats the fish. After 10 minutes, the fish should have changed in color and texture to appear cooked rather than translucent. You can finish the dish and serve at any time after this, or leave to continue "cooking" in the fridge for several hours.

Once ready to serve, cut the avocado in small cubes, salt generously, and toss in with the fish. Clean, trim and thinly slice the radish. Clean the lettuce, leaving the leaves intact, and dry very thoroughly. Taste the fish and add more salt if necessary.

Arrange the lettuce leaves on a platter and mound a couple spoonfuls of ceviche in the center of each leaf. Garnish with a couple slices of radish and a few leaves of cilantro.

ROCK & RAILS SUMMERS IN NIWOT

Lobster roll

Burger with blue cheese, onion rings and heirloom tomato

Kimchi hot dog with sriracha mayo

Caprese salad

Chilled gazpacho

Flatbread with caramelized onions, goat cheese and thyme

Beet salad with avocados, toasted almonds and goat cheese

CHAPTER 8:
Rock & Rails
Summers in Niwot

Although many Niwotians escape the summer heat by heading to the mountains for camping, or hightailing it to the lake house in one of those northern states with a lot of lakes that I always mix up, my experience of summers in Niwot centered around Rock & Rails, the free concert series held half a block from the food truck, at Whistle Stop Park. Every Thursday night, locals and out-of-towners flocked to the park for music, dancing, drinking and cavorting. Waves of people paraded down Murray Street, waving as they passed with promises to return for dinner. Friends stopped by to chat through the pandemonium of the mass exodus at the end of the night.

I stayed open late to provide sustenance to those who could not face the long food lines in the park or those who popped into the Wheel House for a bite and post-concert revelry. Although the food truck was just far enough that the music was a jumble of undistinguishable thrumming, I loved the outpouring of communal joy and vitality on everyone's faces. Folks popped by to share their news, grumble about the crowds, slake their hunger and enjoy the sun setting over the Flatirons.

Late summer is also when the farming communities of Boulder County hit their stride with a glut of colorful and flavorful produce. The tomatoes overflow, the fairytale eggplants delight and the elusive squash blossoms finally appear. Customers and friends often showed up with arms full of excess vegetables from the garden, wondering if I could make use of it. (Always yes!). The wrought-iron blue and red tables outside La Musette were packed with regulars, lounging after a bike ride, meeting up for beers, and enjoying their weekly plein-air La Musette dinner.

Lobster roll

Growing up in California, lobster was not on my radar. I have a powerful memory of Linn cooking live lobsters once. The lobsters' screams as they went into the boiling water are seared in my brain, but I have no recollection of eating them afterwards. It wasn't until I spent time on the East Coast—during and after my college years— that I began to understand the reputation, cultural significance and gastronomical appeal of the lobster. And then, I became obsessed with lobster rolls.

Lobster rolls are one of those foods that are inescapably intertwined with a sense of place. A coastal seafood shack in Maine, an overpriced patio in Montauk, a family-run establishment in Cape Ann. When eating a lobster roll, one can usually smell saltwater in the air and enjoy a sumptuous view of the water. Or, it's summer in Niwot, in the middle of Colorado, and La Musette is open late to feed the local denizens stumbling out of the Rock & Rails concert on a Thursday night.

Unexpectedly, Niwot hosts an annual Lobsterfest. I originally put lobster rolls on the menu the week of the Fest to provide a lobster opportunity to those who could not attend Lobsterfest. After that week, I fielded questions from strangers who were desperately seeking lobster rolls for months. Eventually I caved to the demand and put the lobster roll on the menu for much of the summer.

INGREDIENTS
(Makes 2 generous rolls)

8 oz cooked lobster meat

3 Tbsp mayonnaise

1 lemon, Meyer if available

1 fennel bulb

Salt

Pepper

Brioche hot dog buns with opening slit on top

Butter

Fresh chervil (or dill or tarragon), chiffonaded

Place lobster meat in a large mixing bowl. Wash, dry and zest the lemon (preferably with the cocktail zester pictured on page 34, rather than a microplane, so oils splatter into the bowl). Salt the meat with 1 teaspoon of salt. Add the mayonnaise and juice of the lemon. Toss well to evenly coat the lobster meat in the dressing. Taste and add more salt, lemon or mayonnaise to taste. Set aside in the fridge.

Clean, trim and cut the fennel bulb into quarters. Using a mandoline, make paper-thin slices starting from the thick base. You can either make a quick fennel pickle by adding ½ teaspoon each of salt and sugar, or you can salt and place in ice water to obtain a nice crisp bite to the fennel.

In a cast iron pan on medium heat, add a pat of butter and allow to melt and coat the pan. Gently open the hot dog buns and place on the hot butter to toast until golden brown, about 1 minute. Remove from heat.

When ready to serve, line the butter-toasted bun with fennel slices and then mound the lobster salad mixture on top. Pepper well and garnish with fresh herbs.

Burger with blue cheese, onion rings and heirloom tomato

Ah, the summer burger. I had constant discussions in increasingly loud voices about the summer burger with Stephen, the Wheel House bartender with whom I often discussed menu quandaries. Fundamentally, I do not like cooking the same thing over and over again. Also fundamentally, apparently, according to certain bartenders, folks like to have consistency and know they will always have their favorite dishes available. Eventually I lost the debate so for the last summer I operated, there was a burger on the menu for an astoundingly long stretch. The accoutrements and sides varied, but the burger remained.

I like a thick, well-seasoned burger, served medium rare and showcasing a couple toppings. Tomatoes accompanying a burger should be farm-fresh, full of flavor and sweetness, lightly salted and a thing of beauty. I would never serve an out-of-season, previously refrigerated, tasteless pathetic excuse for a tomato with a burger. I believe in a burger that you look at and have to wonder if it will fit in your mouth, and one for which you have to know where extra napkins are in anticipation of the messy juiciness in your near future. The following is one of my favorite combinations: gooey high-quality blue cheese, rich and tangy onion rings, and bright, sweet and acidic heirloom tomatoes.

BURGER PATTIES

1⅓ pounds 80/20 ground beef (plan ⅓ pound per person)

1 tsp salt

½ tsp powdered shallot or onion (preferable Burlap & Barrel)

½ tsp fish sauce or worcestershire sauce

½ tsp freshly ground pepper

ONION RINGS

2 onion

1 cup milk

1 cup flour

1 tsp salt

½ tsp pepper

1 cup grapeseed oil

TOPPINGS

4 thick slices quality blue cheese like: Cambozola, Forme d'Ambert, Bayley Hazen, Blue d'Auvergne, or Point Reyes Blue

1-2 large heirloom tomatoes, perfectly ripe and thickly sliced

Dijon mustard and/or mayonnaise if desired

Buns, ideally brioche

Mix the ground beef and its seasoning (salt, powdered shallots, fish sauce, pepper) with gloved hands. Fully incorporate the seasoning but do not over-handle the meat. Shape into large hockey pucks, ⅓ pound each, at least 1-inch thick and with neat, patted down edges. Cover and set aside at room temperature for at least 20 minutes while making the onion rings before grilling.

For the onion rings, heat the oil to 350°F. Peel, trim and slice the onions into thick rings. Soak rings in 1 cup of milk. Meanwhile, mix flour, salt and pepper in another bowl. When the oil is hot, move rings from the milk to dredge in the seasoned flour and drop into the hot oil. Fry 4-5 rings at a time or as many as the pan easily accommodates. Flip the rings after one side turns golden. When fully golden, move to a plate lined with a paper towel. Continue until the rings are all fried.

Grill the burgers over high heat, letting the first side cook undisturbed until browned with nice charred grill marks, about 3-4 minutes. Flip and cook the other side. Test for doneness by briefly depressing the center of the burger with a bare finger. For medium rare, the meat should have some give but not be squishy. For more well done, continue cooking, flipping after another few minutes, until the meat is fairly firm to the touch. Add the slab of blue cheese for the last 30 seconds of cooking. If a grill is unavailable, cook on a hot cast iron pan with a lid.

Assemble the burgers on the buns with the toppings piled high.

Kimchi hot dog with sriracha mayo

Once convinced to keep some items on the menu throughout the summer, I brought back the much loved kimchi hot dog. As adults, hot dogs are often relegated to the ballpark, but there is something so satisfying about a high quality dog dressed up with style. This addition also made it easy to accommodate families whose kids prefer a basic dog with ketchup without technically having a kids menu.

As always, use high-quality ingredients. There are local butchers making craft hot dogs these days, as well as some easily available national brands (I like Niman Ranch). For La Musette, I sourced Wagyu hot dogs (the amazing Niwot Market sometimes carries them). Most grocery stores have good options for kimchi now, but to find the pickled daikon radish, check out H-mart or another local Asian shop.

INGREDIENTS

1 package high quality hot dogs

1 package brioche hot dog buns

¼ cup mayonnaise

1 Tbsp sriracha

1 cup kimchi

4-5 long slices yellow pickled daikon radish

Cook the hot dogs on a grill or in a covered frying pan with ¼ cup hot water. Mix the mayonnaise and sriracha until smooth (adjust amount of sriracha to taste). Lightly toast or grill the hot dog buns.

Slather sriracha mayo on the toasted bun and then assemble, nestling the hot dog and a daikon radish on the bun and topping with a generous helping of kimchi.

Caprese salad

I eagerly anticipate the summer's first tomatoes with caprese on my mind. In Niwot, we are fortunate that Mike Dooley grows lovely flavor-filled indoor-grown tomatoes that appear at Niwot Market months before the field tomatoes grace the markets and farm stands. Once field tomatoes are available, I switch to cases of tomatoes from Munsons, heirlooms from Ollin Farms, or gorgeous yellow tomatoes from Kilt Farms.

My love for caprese salad started during my year in Florence. I ate countless versions, usually composed of mozzarella made fresh that day at a local cheese shop and beautiful tomatoes bursting with flavor. Living in New York while I went to law school, I was delighted to discover Joe's Dairy in the Village, where the balls of mozzarella were sometimes still warm from production in the store. With such simple ingredients, this dish is only worth making if you spring for the farm-fresh tomatoes, mozzarella sold in water, single-origin olive oil, and fine balsamic vinegar. Please, for the love of all that is delicious, do not store tomatoes in the fridge, and in fact, they probably should sit out on the counter for a few days to achieve maximum deliciousness.

INGREDIENTS

3 perfectly ripened heirloom tomatoes

1 large ball of fresh mozzarella, buffalo mozzarella, or burrata

Several sprigs basil (also better to store on counter than fridge)

High-quality olive oil

High-quality balsamic vinegar

Salt

Pepper, freshly ground

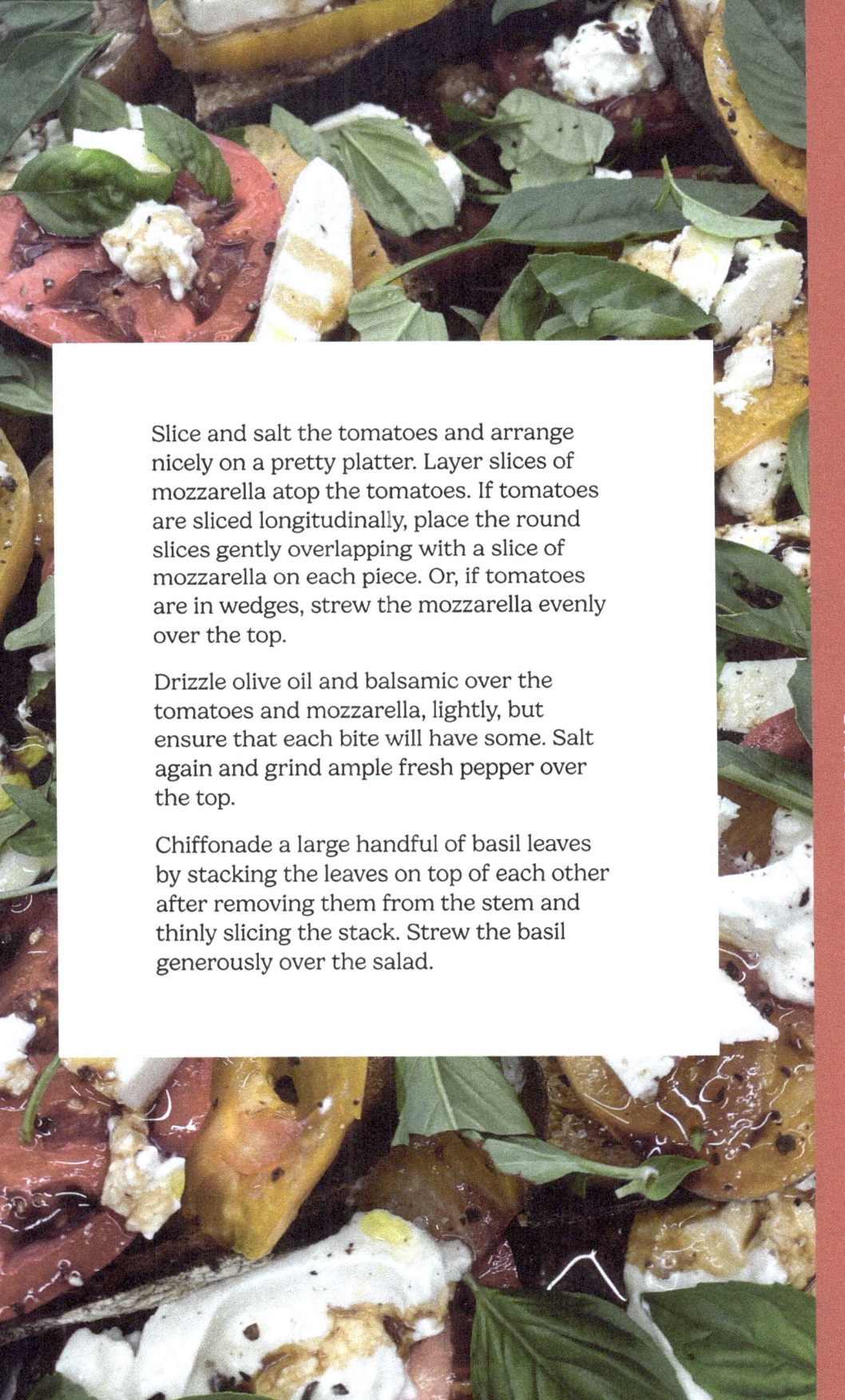

Slice and salt the tomatoes and arrange nicely on a pretty platter. Layer slices of mozzarella atop the tomatoes. If tomatoes are sliced longitudinally, place the round slices gently overlapping with a slice of mozzarella on each piece. Or, if tomatoes are in wedges, strew the mozzarella evenly over the top.

Drizzle olive oil and balsamic over the tomatoes and mozzarella, lightly, but ensure that each bite will have some. Salt again and grind ample fresh pepper over the top.

Chiffonade a large handful of basil leaves by stacking the leaves on top of each other after removing them from the stem and thinly slicing the stack. Strew the basil generously over the salad.

Chilled gazpacho

The sweltering heat of high summer in Boulder County can drive us out of the kitchen and make us crave something cool, refreshing and invigorating. Gazpacho is the solution. The cold Spanish soup is easy to prepare, requires no hot stove, makes use of peak season produce, and best of all, stimulates your senses and sates the yearning for something chilled, savory and delicious.

Although usually thought of as a tomato soup, gazpacho also imparts freshness and crispness from cucumbers and bell peppers. The most important part of this recipe is to use flavorful produce picked at the height of ripeness. You cannot make this in the off-season and please do not try to use bland tasteless tomatoes that have been refrigerated. I never store tomatoes in the fridge. I hate how it changes the texture and halts the development of natural sweetness. Tomatoes should sit on the counter until they are perfectly ripe. Peppers and cucumbers should also come from the farmer's market or a friend's garden. Taste each cucumber before using to be sure they are not bitter. If they are, peel them, slice them and toss with ½ teaspoon each salt sugar. After ten minutes, the salt and sugar should have tempered and removed the bitterness. If the cucumbers are still unbearably bitter, do not use them.

INGREDIENTS

2-3 cucumbers, peeled, salted and sugared if bitter

1 small onion, preferably red or Vidalia

3 cloves garlic

1 large shallot

1 serrano or jalapeño pepper, deseeded

1 Anaheim or bell pepper

6-8 large ripe tomatoes

1-2 Tbsp salt

2 Tbsp sherry vinegar

¼ cup olive oil

1-2 tsp smoked paprika

Clean, peel, trim, deseed and cut ingredients into large chunks. Put everything in the blender, preferably a Vitamix or similarly robust device, if available. Blend until smooth and taste. As necessary, add more salt, olive oil, paprika, vinegar or lemon juice to fine tune the gazpacho to your palate and to accommodate any fluctuations in the profile of the produce used.

Refrigerate for several hours and stir before serving. Serve with a drizzle of olive oil or pesto and freshly ground pepper if desired. Leftover gazpacho can be used as a Bloody Mary mix base, or as a sauce poured over chili rellenos (page 121).

Flatbread with caramelized onions, goat cheese and thyme

Another summer staple at La Musette was flatbread with caramelized onions, goat cheese and thyme. The flattop grill crisped the bottom of the flatbread and the salamander broiler browned the goat cheese. Every slice had a chewy crust with a nice bite to it. The flavors provided a contrast of the sweetness of the onions with the tanginess of the cheese married with the bright green herbaceousness of the thyme.

If you make a large batch of the flatbread dough, it keeps well in the fridge for a few days. With the leftover dough, make plain flatbread for a snack, or throw together a quick pizza with whatever is in the fridge. Or have a pizza party with a variety of toppings presented in an array so guests can assemble their own personal flatbread pizza. A pizza stone on a Green Egg or other grill is perfect for cooking them in an outdoor party setting.

INGREDIENTS

Flatbread dough (page 169)

3 onions

3 Tbsp butter

8 oz fresh soft goat cheese

Several sprigs fresh thyme

Salt

Grapeseed oil

Peel, trim and slice the onions latitudinally and fairly thinly, about ¼ inch wide. Melt the butter over medium heat in a sauce pan. Add the sliced onions and 1 teaspoon salt. Stir to separate and to coat the onions with salt and butter. Reduce the heat to low and place the lid on securely. Stir the onions every five or ten minutes and let cook until the onions have reduced to about a quarter of the volume and have a translucent golden brown hue. This will take at least 40 minutes on the lowest heat setting possible.

If the dough was refrigerated, allow it to sit at room temperature for at least half an hour before using. Separate a chunk of dough and form it into a ball. The size depends on what size flatbread is desired: small discs 3 inches in diameter should be golf ball sized; a personal sized 8-inch flatbread should be baseball sized.

Drizzle a spoonful of grapeseed oil on a flat, clean surface, and push into shape with greased fingers or roll the dough out into a disc, about ½ inch thick. The dough will spring back and shrink a bit; let it rest for a few minutes after the first rolling (covered with plastic or a clean linen kitchen towel so it doesn't dry out), and it will relax enough to keep its shape after rolling out a second time.

Heat a cast iron pan over medium and add a glug of grapeseed oil. Place the flatbread in the pan and cook for about two minutes. The bottom should have golden brown lines and be firm. Flip the dough over and begin layering on toppings. Strew caramelized onions generously on the dough and then add a crumble of goat cheese throughout. Cook the second side of the dough until browned, about another 2 minutes. With a large spatula, transfer the flatbread to a baking sheet and place under the broiler on high for 30 seconds or until the goat cheese turns bubbly and brown.

Remove from heat and slide the flatbread onto a cutting board. Remove the thyme leaves from the sprigs and roughly chop. Sprinkle flatbread with Maldon salt and a generous shower of thyme leaves. Slice and serve.

Beet salad with avocados, toasted almonds and goat cheese

No matter what I am doing with beets, I cook them the same way: roasted in their skins in a Le Creuset pot with an inch of water and then peeled and tossed in vinegar while still warm. They maintain their moisture and earthy sweetness better when steamed in their skins. One of the highest compliments I received at La Musette was when customers would come back to the food truck to report that although they generally hate x, they loved this version of it and cleaned their plate. Beets are apparently something that many people have learned to dislike (rivaled only by eggplant) and it warmed my heart to hear how often non-beet eaters were converted by La Musette salads.

INGREDIENTS

4-5 medium sized beets, rinsed well

1 perfectly ripe avocado

1-2 crisp cucumbers, preferably Armenian, Japanese, or English variety

2 oz fresh chèvre goat cheese

¼ cup raw almonds

Chervil, chives, or fresh thyme

VINAIGRETTE

1 small shallot, minced

1 tsp sugar

½ tsp salt

1 tsp Dijon mustard

2 Tbsp balsamic vinegar

1 Tbsp sherry vinegar

1 Tbsp champagne vinegar

4 Tbsp olive oil

1 tsp chervil, chives or thyme, minced

Roast beets in their skins in a heavy ceramic coated cast iron pot with one inch of water, covered tightly with aluminum foil under the lid, for 60 minutes at 350ºF. Pierce the largest beet with a fork to insure it slides in easily. If not, roast for an additional 30 minutes or until soft. Remove from the oven and peel while running under cold water (use plastic gloves if you do not want red hands for days!) The skins should slip off easily or scrape them off with the back of a paring knife. While still warm, cut in half, salt lightly and toss with 2 tablespoons vinegar. Let cool.

Assemble the vinaigrette in a glass pint canning jar as instructed on page 59 or page 153 for the basic vinaigrette. This variation substitutes balsamic vinegar for the rice vinegar and incorporates the fresh herbs.

Toast the almonds in a cast iron pan until browned on the stovetop or in the oven for 7-12 minutes at 350ºF. Chop roughly. Slice the beets into half moon segments and toss with a pinch of salt and some vinaigrette. Rinse and slice the cucumbers into half moons and toss with a pinch of salt and some vinaigrette. Cube the avocado and salt.

Layer the dressed beets on the bottom of a platter or shallow bowl. Strew the cucumbers over the beets, and then the avocados on top of the cucumbers. Add the goat cheese in clumps and then strew the chopped almonds. Drizzle a little more of the vinaigrette over the salad. Finish with fresh herbs and a final pinch of Maldon salt.

MIDDLE EASTERN MENU

Muhammara

Beet yogurt dip

Hummus

Garlic yogurt

Eggplant caviar

Flatbread

Lemongrass beef skewers

Amy's brick chicken

Bean, tomato and
cucumber salad

Cumin rice

CHAPTER 9:
Middle Eastern Menu

A year after the devastating 2017 wildfires, I set off for a few months of wandering, searching for the seeds of a new existence. The weeks I spent in the Sahara desert were some of the first moments after the fires when I began to feel a spark of inspiration and interest in the future. The intense skies and vast beauty of endless dunes tempted me to consider whether I could have a small food cart in M'hamid, the last town on the edge of the arid wilderness. These early dreams of a small mobile endeavor sharing the food I love with others who wander eventually led me to La Musette.

In addition to my formative time in Morocco, my Middle Eastern cooking is inspired by the beauty of Yotam Ottolenghi and Anissa Helou cookbooks. Their recipes made regular appearances at La Musette. The recipes in this chapter work together for a comprehensive feast but are also good as stand-alone components for a quick weeknight meal.

I love serving a vibrant mezze platter as part of the appetizer spread for an event or as a light and healthy dinner. The various dips are quick to assemble and will last for days as a delightful snack or supplement to subsequent meals. To accompany the dips, serve flatbread and copious crudité: local farm carrots, Armenian cucumbers, bell peppers, Fuji or Honeycrisp apple slices, and whatever else is available, crispy and appetizing. In addition to the recipes below, pick up some olives, feta and dolmas, and make a batch of Paloma's pickled vegetables (page 79) to add to the platter.

Muhammara

Muhammara is a vibrant and flavorful dip featuring charred bell peppers and toasted walnuts. Unlike many recipes, which rely on bread for texture, I use tortilla chips to keep it gluten-free.

INGREDIENTS

4 red or orange bell peppers

¼ cup toasted walnuts

1 Tbsp olive oil

1 clove garlic, smashed and salted

1 shallot or scallion

1 tsp fresh lemon juice

¼ of a preserved lemon or the zest of a lemon, preferably Meyer

Handful of tortilla chips

Pinch of cumin, urfa chili and/or Aleppo chili to taste

Salt, to taste (but at least 1-2 tsp)

Blacken the bell peppers under the broiler, on the grill, or directly over the flames of a gas stove, turning often with tongs. The peppers should be blackened throughout the exterior, but to prevent it from burning through the flesh, turn the pepper as soon as it is blackened. Once the peppers are properly charred, put them in a container with a lid or a closed paper bag so they can continue to steam cook. When cooled, peel the charred skin off and scrape any seeds with fingers or the back of a knife. Do not wash the peppers after cooking, as the flecks of char are part of the smokey flavor.

Put all the ingredients into a food processor and run for several minutes until smooth. Add more oil or a drizzle of water if the muhammara is too thick. Adjust lemon juice, salt and spices to reflect your palate.

Serve with a zhuzh of olive oil and a sprinkle of silk or urfa chili.

Another favorite addition to the mezze platter is charred bell peppers in garlic oil. After peeling the blackened bell peppers, thinly sliced into strips, cover with olive oil and stir in a teaspoon of minced salted garlic. Add a few strips of peppers to the platter near the garlic yogurt sauce. If covered in oil, they will last for days.

Beet yogurt dip

This beet yogurt dip delights guests for its striking beauty and deliciousness. The initial cooking of the beets—roasted in their skins and then tossed with salt and vinegar—is how I prepare my beets for salads as well. The beets develop a silky texture, retaining moisture in their skins, and the vinegar helps to balance their sweetness. The vinegar also helps preserve them so you can have beets available for 5 or 6 days in the fridge, ready to whip up as a quick side with goat cheese and nuts, add to a green or citrus salad, or throw together with yogurt as below.

INGREDIENTS

3-4 medium sized red beets

2 Tbsp rice or apple cider vinegar

2 cups Greek yogurt (I use Fage 5%)

2 cloves garlic, smashed and salted with a squeeze of lemon juice

1 tsp ground cumin

½ tsp Kashmiri chili, Aleppo chili, Urfa chili, or other chili powder

1 Tbsp pomegranate or date molasses (or substitute 2 dates or 1 tsp honey)

1-3 tsp salt

2-5 Tbsp olive oil

1-4 tsp lemon juice

Roast the beets in their skins in a heavy ceramic or cast iron pot in 1 inch of water, covered tightly with aluminum foil under the lid, for 60 minutes at 350°. Pierce the largest beet with a fork to ensure it slides in easily. If not, roast for an additional 30 minutes or until soft. Remove from the oven and peel while running under cold water. While still warm, cut in half, salt lightly and toss with 2 tablespoons of vinegar. Let cool.

Place all the ingredients in a food processor, using the lower end of amounts for salt, lemon juice and olive oil to start, and blend until smooth. Taste and adjust, using more salt, olive oil and/or lemon juice to obtain the flavor and consistency you prefer.

Hummus

There are so many variations of hummus available commercially, so it's hard to say whether it's worth making a homemade version. If you have one you love, buying it is obviously easier. The benefit of making it, however, is that you can achieve your perfect ratio of tahini, garlic and lemon juice and the texture of your choice. So if you have never quite found the right hummus, start here and experiment.

INGREDIENTS

2 cups cooked chickpeas (1 cup dried)

2-5 cloves garlic, smashed and salted (or spring green garlic, roasted garlic or confited garlic)

Zest and juice of 1 lemon, preferably Meyer

¼-½ cup tahini

1 tsp ground cumin

3 Tbsp olive oil

Chickpea water

Salt

If using dried chickpeas rather than canned, soaked overnight, and then cooked for 30 minutes until tender in plenty of water with 1 teaspoon salt. Strain and reserve the cooking liquid for the hummus.

If you remove the translucent skin from the beans, the hummus will be silker. It is a hassle, so I only occasionally make the effort.

Pulse the garlic, 1 teaspoon lemon juice, and 1 teaspoon salt in a food processor. Let this sit for a few minutes to pull the bitterness out of the garlic, and then add the chickpeas and about ¼ cup of chickpea cooking liquid or water. Mix in the processor. Add ¼ cup tahini and restart the processor. Slowly drizzle more chickpea liquid or water in as the ingredients blend together. Add olive oil and cumin and start tasting and tinkering with the hummus. Slowly add more tahini, lemon juice, salt, olive oil, water and cumin until the flavor and consistency is what you desire. Taste after each addition and stop when you inadvertently mumble "mmm!" to yourself.

The hummus will firm up as it sets, so add a little more water and stir before serving if needed. Serve with a drizzle of olive oil.

Garlic yogurt

This garlic yogurt takes 5 minutes to make and is referred to as "magic sauce" by my friend Abby. It embodies the idea that the whole is greater than the sum of the parts and shows the transformative nature of cooking. The sauce is great as a mezze dip, but it also dresses up any variety of grilled meats or fish. Add some fresh herbs or other spices to complement whatever is on the table tonight.

INGREDIENTS

2 cloves garlic

1 pint Greek yogurt (Fage 5% brand is my favorite)

1 lemon

Cumin

Salt

Sugar

In a mortar and pestle, pound the garlic with a generous pinch of salt, a pinch of ground cumin, and pinch of sugar until it forms a smooth paste. Add 1 teaspoon lemon juice, pound until incorporated and let sit for 5 minutes. Stir this paste into the Greek yogurt. Taste, and then add more salt, sugar, cumin, or lemon juice if needed to taste.

Eggplant caviar

Eggplant caviar is a vegan dip that has converted many an eggplant-wary customer into a grudging fan. I first encountered it in the beautiful cookbook Chez Panisse Vegetables, and have adapted it from there. Named for its similarity in appearance to caviar, the balsamic vinegar and copious fresh herbs transform the vegetable into a sophisticated dip that is nothing like the more familiar smokey baba ghanoush. I love baba ghanoush but have found it to be a somewhat polarizing mezze for a group (especially the eggplant averse). The eggplant caviar, on the other hand, generally dazzles and surprises.

INGREDIENTS

1 large Italian globe eggplant	Salt
Olive oil	Sugar
2 cloves garlic	2 Tbsp balsamic vinegar
2 shallots	¼ cup fresh basil, cilantro, and/or dill

Peel and cube the eggplant and then toss with a generous coating of olive oil and salt. Spread onto a lined baking sheet and roast at 350°F for 15-25 minutes, depending on the size of the cubes. The eggplant should be cooked thoroughly and soft enough to mash with a fork. Transfer to a metal mixing bowl and mash well with said fork.

While baking, assemble the other ingredients: finely mince the garlic and shallots and let macerate with a teaspoon each of salt and sugar for a few minutes. Cover with 2 tablespoons balsamic vinegar and let sit until the eggplant is ready. Chiffonade the fresh herbs.

Mix the smashed eggplant with the garlic/shallot/balsamic until well incorporated. Adjust salt, olive oil and vinegar to taste. There may be enough olive oil from cooking, but add more if needed to achieve the right vinegar and oil balance. Once the eggplant is cool, stir in the fresh herbs.

Flatbread

This recipe is adapted from the beautiful cookbook Feasts: Food of the Islamic World by Anissa Helou. Prior to its publication, Amy recipe-tested much of the cookbook for Anissa up at Sky. Lore and I would eagerly await each creation like poorly trained begging dogs. Among our favorites were the "hot pockets" (Moroccan r'ghayef)—multilayered bread stuffed with cumin, paprika and ground lamb or beef. I adapted the hot pockets dough and use it for all manner of recipes, including for flatbreads, pizza, perogis, empanadas, and pigs in a blanket. It's quick to assemble and versatile, and lasts for a couple days in the fridge.

As an accompaniment to a mezze plate, I serve the flatbread plain, sliced into strips as a vehicle for dips.

INGREDIENTS

1 cup regular wheat flour

1 cup semolina flour

If you only have regular flour, use two cups total, but the texture of the dough won't be as pliable as when you use both types. It's worth finding semolina for it.

½ tsp dry yeast

1 tsp salt

⅞ cup warm water

1 Tbsp grape seed oil

Add all the ingredients together in a stand mixer bowl and mix at speed 1 or 2 with the dough hook. The dough should come together after a few minutes, but if it is still too dry, add another teaspoon of oil or water until it assembles.

Knead with the dough hook for 5 minutes after the dough comes together. Cover with a clean kitchen towel for 10 minutes, then remove and knead again at speed 1 for an additional two minutes. Put the dough in an oiled bowl and cover with plastic wrap directly draped on the dough. The dough will be ready to use in half an hour, or can be refrigerated and used over the next several days.

Pull or cut a portion of the dough, about 50 grams or a tenth of the total, and shape into a flattened disc. On an oiled surface, using your fingers, spread the dough into a circle about the size of a corn tortilla, about ½-inch thick. Let it rest for a couple minutes and then enlarge the disc by pushing it out away from the center with your fingers.

Heat a cast iron pan to medium and coat with 2 teaspoons grapeseed oil. Place the disc on the pan and cook for 2 minutes per side, until golden brown marks appear and the flatbread slightly puffs up and is cooked through. Serve warm.

After preparing the dough, you can add any manner of ingredients to make your flatbread into a quick pizza. See Flatbread with Caramelized onions, goat cheese and thyme (page 151) for instructions.

Lemongrass beef skewers

These lemongrass beef skewers can be the centerpiece of a summery meal, prepared with a refreshing punch in hand while entertaining friends on the back patio. Most of the work is done in advance and they take only a few minutes on the grill to be ready to eat as finger food with a plate of tomato and eggplant salad, some flatbread and a few mezze dips. Or bake off a tray and include in a mezze platter for a party.

For a quick and delightful summer punch, mix Clementino Della Piana liqueur from Compania and Cere's guava punch over ice.

INGREDIENTS

1 pound ground beef

2 Tbsp finely diced lemongrass from the bottom white portion of the stalk

2 tsp ground cumin

¼ cup finely chopped scallions

2 cloves garlic, minced and salted

1 tsp sugar

1 Tbsp fish sauce

1 Tbsp oyster sauce

1 tsp salt

1 tsp freshly ground black or white pepper

1 tsp cornstarch

1 jar grape leaves in brine or water

Mix all the ingredients together with gloved hands until fully incorporated. If you prefer a smoother texture, you can put all the ingredients besides the beef in a food processor, skipping the dicing and mincing of each ingredient, but still cutting the lemongrass into smaller chunks so it will process. Then mix the resultant sauce into the beef.

Form small logs about the size of a dolma or C battery. Rinse the grape leaves in a bowl of water and lay out flattened on a large area, about 9 at a time. Place a log of beef in the lower center, toward the stem area, of each grape leaf, tuck each of the two outer sides over, and snuggly roll it up. If skewering, place three in a row and pierce all three with two skewers, each about a third of the way from the outer edges. If baking, oil a baking sheet and line the logs up with about half an inch between them. Brush olive oil on the grape leaves and grill, 2 minutes per side on medium high heat until firm to the touch, or bake at 400°F for 9 minutes.

Serve with garlic yogurt.

Amy's brick chicken

My father's partner, Amy Dencler, is a sublime chef. She is currently Chef at Chez Panisse Restaurant and presides over every kitchen she graces with an unparalleled serene competence. Most picky eaters I know have an "Amy exception" where, no matter how much they dislike something, they will try it and enjoy it anyway if Amy is at the helm. One of the great fortunes of my life has been the times I have spent in the kitchen and at the table with Amy. Of the incalculable lessons I have learned from Amy, the chicken recipe below remains a favorite.

Casual dinners on the porch at Sky featuring Amy's brick chicken helped transform me from a person who refused to eat chicken into one whose eyes gleamed anytime I saw her deboning a chicken thigh. In fact, the seeds for many of my recipes likely originated from late summer twilight Amy dinners on the porch.

Brick chicken, from the Italian "pollo al mattone," is literally cooked underneath a brick. The weight of the brick flattens the meat so it has all of its surface area in contact with the heat and cooks quickly, sealing

in the juices and developing a crispy skin. The texture is unparalleled and the prep and cook time are both brief, making this a perfect component to a quick weeknight meal. Skin-on, boneless thighs are sometimes difficult to source, but most butchers, even at standard grocery stores, are willing to debone the thighs for you if you are not up for it.

INGREDIENTS

2 deboned, skin-on chicken thighs

2 tsp salt

½ tsp whole peppercorns

1 tsp coriander seeds

1 tsp Aleppo chili

1 tsp whole cumin seeds

Grapeseed or other high temperature-friendly oil

In a mortar and pestle, combine the salt and all the spices and pound until there are no longer any whole seeds. The mixture should be a rough chunky rub rather than a fine powder. Liberally sprinkle both sides of the chicken thighs with the rub and let sit for half an hour on a covered plate outside of the fridge.

Heat a cast iron pan to medium hot and pour a generous glug of oil into the hot pan. Place the chicken thighs, skin side down, in the hot oil and cover with parchment paper. Weigh down with a brick or two, or another slightly smaller cast iron pan weighted down with something heavy.

Let the chicken cook for about 4 minutes and then peek under the parchment to ensure that the skin is golden and crispy. If not, turn the heat up slightly and allow to cook for another minute. When golden and crispy, remove the brick and parchment, flip the thighs, and then replace the parchment (same side down) and the brick. Cook this side for about 2 minutes. You can cut into a thigh to make sure it is cooked through—a tiny bit of pink is fine, but if it looks translucent like raw chicken, keep cooking for another couple of minutes.

Transfer the cooked thighs to a clean plate or cutting board. Let sit for a couple minutes before slicing in half-inch thick pieces and serving.

Serve with garlic yogurt and the marinated charred bell peppers from page 160.

Bean, tomato and cucumber salad

A summer salad with fresh local vegetables elevates any meal. With such a simple fare, the quality of ingredients is critical. If you don't have access to local heirloom tomatoes, multicolored cherry tomatoes are usually the most flavorful substitute. Do not use refrigerated pale flavorless tomatoes in the winter for this recipe. I beg you.

For cucumbers, in a regular grocery store, Armenian, Persian or English have a better crunch and flavor than standard watery cucumbers. If you have a local farmers market or farm stand, look for lemon cucumbers (select the pale green small ones and avoid those with bright yellow skin — they are too old), or pale green Poona Kheera slicing cucumbers. In general, the smaller younger cucumbers will have better flavor and crunch and be less likely to be bitter, seedy or watery.

For beans, try to source dried Rancho Gordo beans. I especially love their large Corona beans for this recipe, although the smaller flageolet and Great Northern are also nice. If you don't have time to soak and cook the beans, or don't want the extra work, there are nice cooked beans in glass jars that are preferable to the canned varieties, although canned works in a pinch as well. Drain and rinse canned beans.

INGREDIENTS

½ pound dried Corona or other beans

Bay leaf

½ onion

2 cucumbers, sliced

2 large heirloom tomatoes, trimmed and cut into wedges

¼ cup pickled onions

1 shallot

¼ cup vinegar

1 tsp Dijon mustard

¼ cup olive oil

Salt

Basil leaves

Soak dried beans overnight and cook in ample water seasoned with salt, a glug of olive oil, a bay leaf and half of an onion until soft. Let cool.

Assemble the vinaigrette, as on page 59 or page 153.

Strain the beans and toss with pickled onions, sliced cucumbers, and sliced heirloom tomatoes. Dress with vinaigrette. Salt and pepper generously. Add whole basil leaves to garnish.

Cumin rice

A Middle Eastern dinner at La Musette usually included a flavorful rice dish, like a tahdig, a pilaf, or a mujadara. I've included the simple cumin rice recipe here, as it works well for a simple weeknight like many of the dishes in this chapter.

INGREDIENTS

½ onion

1 tsp cumin seeds

1 cup medium grain white rice

1¾ cups water or chicken broth

Salt

Olive oil

Crispy fried shallots (storebought or sliced and fried in grapeseed oil)

Sauté the onion in olive oil with ½ teaspoon salt until soft. Add the cumin seeds and stir. After about 30 seconds, add the rice and stir until coated in oil. Pour in 1¾ cups water or broth, cover, and turn down heat to the lowest setting. Alternatively toss everything in your rice cooker. If cooking on the stovetop, check after 20 minutes. Fluff and top with crispy shallots.

CHAPTER 10:

ASIAN INFLUENCES

CHAPTER 10:
Asian Influences

I love Japanese cuisine: umami reigns supreme, but the flavors are still subtle and delicate. It incorporates high quality ingredients with fundamental techniques and offers an array of taste-dazzling morsels.

I first learned to cook Japanese fare from Tomoka Moriya Wesely, my quasi-sister who lived with my family as an exchange student twenty-some years ago. I have since visited Tomoka, her husband Adam, and their son Shia in various regions in Japan, eating, learning and cooking my way through more of the cuisine. I was also fortunate to become close with and learn much from the amazing chef Ryoji Kajikawa, a yakitori master roaming the Los Angeles scene. Their influence, as well as later travels through Malaysia, South Korea, Thailand, Singapore, and Vietnam, often found its way onto La Musette's menus.

My approach to cooking cuisines from cultures that I appreciate but am not a member of is one of balancing. I want to share my love and respect of the food and culture but I do not want to appropriate or take resources that should go to folks of that culture in the industry. In Niwot, we are lucky to have Sachi Sushi in the Niwot market, with the supremely talented Chef Tsukasa. Anytime I featured global cuisines at La Musette, I was mindful of not stepping on toes or creating any competition for the local establishments whose expertise and authenticity in these areas should be elevated and respected.

Miso braised pork and root vegetable stew

This recipe was inspired by an incandescent stew that Tomoka made for a work lunch at Sky during a wine-labeling day about twenty years ago. When I asked Tomoka how to make it many years later, she didn't remember the lunch, so I improvised this recipe based on my memories. It changes every time I make it but it is always satisfying.

INGREDIENTS

1½ pounds pork shoulder, cut into 1-inch cubes and lightly salted

3 Tbsp sesame oil

1 onion, diced

3 Tbsp minced fresh ginger (2 inches of a thick root)

½ cup sake

2 Tbsp soy sauce

2-3 cups peeled and cubed assortment of root vegetables, in any combination, such as:

- Carrots

- Daikon

- Burdock

- Sweet Potato

- Potato

- Radish

- Parsnips

Dashi (or chicken broth or water)

¼ cup miso paste, preferably a combination of white and red

In a heavy-bottomed pan, heat the sesame oil and sauté the cubed pork shoulder until browned. Add the diced onion and sauté for a few minutes until translucent. Add minced ginger and stir for another minute. Deglaze, scraping any brown bits from the pan, with ½ cup sake. Cook for a minute or so and then add the soy sauce.

Add the cubed root vegetables and dashi (hot water soaked with bonito flakes and/or kombu seaweed for 20 mins and then strained), water, or chicken broth to cover the stew contents by 2 inches. Nestle red and white miso in pockets, ½ spoonful at a time, throughout.

Slowly simmer for two hours over low heat with a lid slightly ajar, until the meat is tender. Adjust for flavor before serving, adding more miso paste or soy sauce if under seasoned.

Serve over rice, beside rice, or solo.

Miso glazed salmon

One of my favorite things about the grocers in Japan is the veritable cornucopia of their seafood departments. You'll see every variety of freshly caught fish, available in several formats, usually including sashimi grade, sun-dried, and miso marinated. I serve this salmon as a small plate of fish for breakfast, accompanied by the usual Japanese breakfast smorgasbord, to satisfy the umami craving I awaken to and provide a protein-fueled boost for the day ahead. Or as a centerpiece for a light evening meal. Or as a component to a bento box style lunch. Basically, I can eat miso glazed fish anytime, day or night, hot or cold!

The shio koji used as a marinade in the recipe below is a magical ingredient. Look for it at Japanese-centered Asian markets or order it online. Look for either the pouches of chunky white liquid or a bottle of clear strained liquid. It seasons and tenderizes the fish, and prevents it from drying out even if slightly over cooked. If shio koji is unavailable, omit it and instead lightly salt the fish.

This is an easy dish to prepare and have on hand: use any flaky fish (like salmon, halibut, black cod), keep a batch of miso butter in the fridge (it easily lasts for a month and freezes even longer) and if you can source the koji, marinated pieces of fish will last in the fridge for a few days or can be portioned and frozen for future use.

INGREDIENTS

1 pound salmon filet, cut into 4 portions

¼ cup shio koji

½ cup (1 stick) unsalted butter, softened

½ cup miso paste (any types; white miso is common; sweet miso and barley miso are also nice variations)

To make the miso butter, combine the softened butter with the miso paste. Mix together with a rubber spatula until completely integrated. Store excess in the fridge.

Add the shio koji to the salmon filet pieces, ensuring they are fully coated. Return marinated fish to the fridge for at least an hour, or up to a few days. The shio koji will help preserve the raw fish longer in the fridge.

When ready to cook, slather 1-2 tablespoons of the room temperature miso butter on each piece of fish. Roast in a 425°F oven on a baking tray for 8-12 minutes, depending on the thickness of the fish. Using a fork, peek inside the thickest section of fish to ensure it is cooked through and has lost its translucence. The miso glaze should turn golden brown. If needed, turn the broiler on for 30 seconds to finish browning the miso glaze.

Soy pickled eggs

One of the joys of traveling to Japan is how every bowl of ramen you consume there comes topped with a beautiful egg. Ramen eggs are always perfectly cooked: hard boiled but with a vibrant orange yolk that remains slightly gooey and seasoned with an umami rich soy-based brine.

At La Musette, I married the ramen egg with a southern deviled egg for an irresistible bar snack or party tray. The soy pickled eggs can garnish ramen or a bento box, be served at a dinner party, or pair nicely as a snack for beer or a cocktail. Tom, the proprietor of Niwot Liquors, and Alan, co-proprietor of Victory Motors, were two of the biggest fans of soy pickled eggs so I would set aside a few servings for them whenever the menu called for a batch.

INGREDIENTS

12 eggs

¾ cup low-sodium soy sauce or tamari (tamari will make it gluten-free)

3 Tbsp mirin

2 Tbsp rice vinegar

1 Tbsp chili crunch (try the local Kream Kimchi Chili Crunch or Rising Tiger Jank)

Any variety of toppings: fried shallots, sesame oil, more chili crunch, diced anchovies, urfa chili, Aleppo chili, sriracha mayo, pickled sansho, fresh peppercorns, shiso or perilla leaf, chiffonaded

Boil the eggs. To boil your eggs to the perfect texture, you need to practice and experiment. Egg size, elevation, quantity of water and quantity of eggs will all be relevant. Aim for an egg where the white is completely solid and the yolk is not runny, but not entirely firm either. Some call it a 7-minute egg; in Niwot with elevation reducing boiling temperature, I find that 8½ or even 9 minutes are necessary. The water should be at a low boil before adding the eggs and the eggs should be at room temperature. Use the oldest eggs in your fridge; just as fresher eggs are key to poaching, older eggs where the whites have broken down make better boiled eggs that are easier to peel.

Gently place half the eggs in boiling water with a spider or slotted spoon and set an alarm for 8½ minutes. When the alarm goes off, immediately transfer the eggs to an ice water bath to stop the cooking. Peel the eggs under the water as soon as they are cool enough to touch. Cut one in half to ensure the yolk consistency is as desired and adjust the cooking time of the second batch if necessary. (Snack on it with a dollop of chili crunch and soy sauce).

Combine the light soy sauce, mirin, vinegar and chili crunch. Submerge the eggs in the marinade for at least 2 hours and up to 5 days. To serve, cut in half, spoon a bit of the marinade on top each half and garnish with any combination of the suggested toppings (or your own). Drizzling sesame or chili oil on the yolk will protect it from drying out if you are putting a tray of eggs out at a party.

Potato, onion and turnip miso soup

Tomoka always says that miso soup should have no more than three ingredients added to the base. The variety of the miso soup components that she showcases in the Japanese breakfast that I demand every time I visit is astounding: turnip greens, mizuna, snow peas, maitake mushrooms, enoki, pioppino mushrooms, shimeji mushrooms, oyster mushrooms, negi onions, turnips, cabbage, potatoes, soft tofu, fried tofu, etc., etc., but only three items are allowed per soup.

This combination of potato, onion and turnip is one of my favorites. I substitute fried tofu from the freezer if hakurei turnips are not in season (or not in the fridge) but the combination of potato and onion is fairly common in my kitchen. The additional umami the onions impart to the dashi cures hangovers.

Miso soup is one of the dishes that I make when I have nothing to eat in the house and do not feel like cooking. Stocking up on miso paste and bonito flakes at an Asian market—both of which have a long shelf life in the fridge—makes miso soup a quick and easy dish for breakfast or dinner that can be ready in 20 minutes.

INGREDIENTS

¼ cup packed bonito flakes (or a loose fistful)

4-6 cups water

1-2 yellow potatoes

1 small onion

6 small hakurei turnips

¼ cup miso paste, white, red or a combination

Place the bonito flakes in a pot with the water and bring up to warm, but turn off the heat before it boils. After 10-20 minutes, remove the bonito flakes with a strainer.

While waiting for the bonito to infuse the dashi, peel and cube the potatoes and trim, peel and slice the onion latitudinally. Peel and quarter the turnips, keeping the greens intact if they are nice. Soak turnips in water to clean any dirt from the stem area.

As soon as you remove the bonito flakes, add the potato and onion to the dashi and heat up a low boil. Simmer for 10 minutes until the potato is cooked through. Add the turnips and cook for an additional 3 minutes. Remove the heat from the pan. Once the dashi has stopped boiling, add the miso paste, pushing it through a strainer barely submerged in the hot liquid. Take care not to boil the soup after adding the miso paste, as that will ruin the texture and health benefits of the miso paste.

Serve immediately or keep warm under a boil.

Korean BBQ short ribs

Galbi marinated, thinly-cut beef short ribs are one of the paragons of Korean cuisine. The marbled meat with its chewy collagen tendons near the bone is the perfect vehicle for the complex flavors of the marinade and the quick grilling over high heat provides the crowning element of caramelized seared bits. There's a reason that most Korean dramas have a scene of one character begging, betting, or demanding to be taken out for barbecued beef.

At La Musette, the galbi short ribs flew out the door anytime I ran a Korean menu. I usually served them with a variety of banchan sides, rice and perilla (sesame) leaves so customers could make their own wraps, but they are also great for a summer barbecue or quick weeknight meal. The marinade will preserve the meat in the fridge and can be left on for hours or days.

INGREDIENTS

1-2 pounds thinly-sliced flanken style short ribs (ideal thinness is best procured from Asian markets); plan for at least 2 slices (each with 3-4 ribs) per person

⅓ cup soy sauce

¼ cup brown sugar

¼ cup mirin

¼ cup sake

1 Tbsp toasted sesame oil

2 tsp whole peppercorns

2 Tbsp gochujang paste

1 medium yellow onion, peeled and trimmed

1 apple or pear, cut off its core

2-inch piece of fresh ginger, peeled

2 tsp sesame seeds

1 Tbsp ketjap manis dark soy sauce, if available

For best results, use the edge of a regular spoon turned upside-down to peel ginger root rather than a knife or peeler.

Place all the ingredients except for the meat in a blender and purée until smooth. Pour the marinade over the ribs and ensure they are all evenly coated. Refrigerate until ready to grill.

Grill over high heat, flipping after a couple minutes, until both sides are marked with some caramelized charred parts. Serve as long strips or cut into bite-sized pieces using kitchen scissors to cut between each rib.

Korean vegetable pancake

Jeon or Korean savory pancakes, are a staple of bar food, Korean BBQ menus, rainy day fare in K-dramas, and part of traditional holiday and memorial tables. The term applies to single ingredients breaded and fried, as well as the pancake made with mixed thinly-sliced ingredients, like here. You can add sliced shrimp, pork, or other protein, by searing it in the pan before adding the pancake batter, or stick to the vegetarian recipe below. Scallion-heavy pancakes, or pajeon, are a common variant, but I prefer this cabbage and mixed vegetable version.

At La Musette, I served a large, plate sized pancake with shrimp or pork as a main dish or small vegetarian pancakes as a banchan (side dish) with other Korean fare. I love the versatility — you can use whatever vegetables are on hand — and how it works either as a shared snack with drinks if company stops in unexpectedly, or as a solo dinner when it's past dinnertime and you don't know what to cook.

PANCAKE

1 bunch scallion, cleaned and sliced

1 yellow onion, peeled and sliced

2 carrots, peeled and grated

2 large tokyo turnips or 1 large purple radish, peeled and mandolined

1 stalk green garlic, minced; or 2-3 cloves garlic, minced

1-inch piece of ginger, peeled and minced

1 cup water or dashi

1 cup flour

2 eggs

Salt

Sesame oil

PAJEON SAUCE

2 Tbsp rice vinegar

2 Tbsp water

6 Tbsp soy sauce

1 Tbsp gochujang

2 garlic cloves

½-inch piece of ginger, peeled

1 tsp sesame seeds

Grate or thinly slice all the vegetables into a large bowl. Toss with 2 teaspoons salt and set aside. When ready to mix with pancake batter, squeeze liquid out vegetables.

For the pajeon sauce, pound the garlic and ginger together with a pinch of salt in a mortar and pestle. Once it has created a paste, add the gochujang paste and pound together. Add the vinegar, water and soy sauce and stir together with the pestle. Move to serving dish and add the sesame seeds.

Continue making the pancakes by whisking together the dashi, flour, eggs, and a pinch of salt. Drain any water from the vegetables and mix together with the batter.

Heat a cast iron pan and add a glug of sesame oil. Add pancake batter to the pan, either as one large pancake, about 1 inch thick, extending 1 inch away from the side of the pan, or as 3 smaller pancakes with an inch of space between them. Cook for a few minutes until the bottom is set, but not crisped or brown, flip the pancake, and flatten with your spatula. Cook this side well until golden brown, then flip again and finish browning the first side. If you like a crispy edge, add more oil as you flip so each side fries up.

Serve hot, sliced like a pizza, with pajeon sauce.

Samgyetang inspired chicken congee

I came late to the party for Korean food but when the pandemic hit, like many, I fell into a K-drama rabbit hole. I started learning Korean, which eventually developed into an appreciation for K-pop and an obsession with Korean cuisine.

In 2024, I finally visited Korea for the first time. Beyond the basics of domestic Korean restaurants, my extensive consumption of Korean media had driven my interest in less familiar culinary forays: ttoebokki, hotteok, beer with all manner of fried pancake jeon, late night fishcakes on skewers, cold noodles, hot noodles, samgeytang chicken stew.

The four days I spent wandering solo in Seoul were filled with one gastronomic surprise and delight after another. I found myself in an alley known for a particular type of chicken stew and peered into windows as I walked up and down the alley, passing 30 restaurants all specializing in that one dish, but was too intimidated to venture into any of them. Every table had a crowd of at least four people sharing the dish and I felt unusually ill-at-ease dining solo (something I usually enjoy). Frustrated with my failure to be bold, I slipped into a hole-in-the-wall in the next alley over — this was grilled fish alley — broke out my elementary Korean, and ordered a feast of grilled fish, tofu soup, banchan and plenty of soju to soften the self-recriminations. The next day I headed to a district known for samgyetang chicken stew and finally experienced the revelation of the soul-nourishing chicken, ginseng and rice stew.

The traditional dish has a whole chicken served over soft gelatinous rice with a rich broth and crunchy garnish, but when I tried to serve it at La Musette, one customer returned it to the kitchen, intimidated by the whole chicken and requesting I serve it with, at most, half of a chicken. After that, I created this version, which is basically a simplified rice congee inspired by samgyetang.

INGREDIENTS

2 pounds skinless boneless chicken thighs

3-inch piece of fresh ginger, peeled and sliced into coins

4 garlic cloves, peeled

1 piece ginseng root, if available (or a ginseng tea bag)

6 jujubes (if unavailable from Asian market, substitute pitted dates)

2 cups glutinous sweet rice (or sushi rice)

8 cups chicken stock or water

¼ cup toasted sunflower seeds

¼ cup toasted pumpkin seeds

¼ cup fried shallots

¼ scallion or spring onion greens, chiffonaded

Salt

Soy sauce

Sesame oil

Salt the chicken thighs. In a heavy-bottomed pot, a slow cooker, or a rice cooker, heat 2 tablespoons of sesame oil. Add the ginger slices, the chicken thighs, and the whole garlic cloves. Sauté together for a few minutes. Add the jujubes, the whole ginseng root, and the rice. (If you cannot source ginseng root, brew a cup of ginseng tea and add it to the liquid).

Cover with 8 cups of chicken stock or water and cook on low for at least 2 hours. If using a rice cooker, you may need to add the liquid in two steps and run the machine at least twice on the porridge setting.

Taste for seasoning. The chicken should be falling apart tender and the rice should be soft and losing its shape when done.

Serve in a bowl with a drizzle of sesame oil and soy sauce, garnished with sunflower seeds, pumpkin seeds, fried shallots, and green onion slices, or any combination thereof.

Satay chicken with peanut sauce

Traveling through Singapore and Malaysia with the Yee family, my Boulder friends who initially coaxed me into moving to Colorado, was a satay celebration. Everywhere we went we were delighted to find street cart vendors with marinated meats on skewers, open flames, and flavorful peanut sauces.

The version I often featured at La Musette was an entrée served on rice, garnished with fresh bean sprouts and cilantro. I adapted the peanut sauce recipe from the Vietnamese grandmother of Shen, one of my teenaged food truck assistants, and it became one of my most popular menu items.

INGREDIENTS

¾ cup peeled and trimmed shallots

3 large garlic cloves

1-2 Tbsp chili crunch

2 Tbsp brown sugar

1 Tbsp salt

1 tsp Kashmiri chili powder

2 tsp powdered cumin

1-inch fresh turmeric root, peeled, or 1 tsp powdered turmeric

1 small fresh apple or pear, peeled and cored

2 Tbsp ketjap manis dark soy sauce

¼ cup sesame oil

¼ cup shallot oil or grapeseed oil

1-2 pounds skinless boneless chicken thighs (1 or 1½ thighs per person)

1 package bean sprouts, cleaned and trimmed

1 bunch fresh cilantro leaves, rinsed

¼ cup peanuts, roasted

2 cups jasmine rice, cooked (1 cup uncooked)

1 cup peanut butter

½ cup hoisin sauce

1 Tbsp chili crunch

1/2-2 cups water

To assemble the satay marinade, put the first 12 ingredients in a blender and purée until smooth. Taste and adjust saltiness if necessary. Slice chicken thighs into thin strips, about ½-inch thick. Put the chicken in the marinade, stirring well to ensure every piece is full coated. Cover and refrigerate for at least an hour or ideally overnight.

For the peanut sauce, combine the peanut butter, hoisin and chili crunch in a small saucepan and heat. Slowly pour the water in while stirring. The water will make the other ingredients form an emulsion, thin and smoothen the sauce, and change the color from dark brown to a glossy tan color. Add as much water as is necessary to obtain these three goals, starting with ½ cup. If the sauce keeps breaking with the oil separating, add more water and blend with an immersion blender. If the sauce later begins to dry out, thicken or separate, add more water to return it to the desired consistency. The sauce will keep for a couple weeks in the fridge and goes great with cucumber and carrot sticks for a quick snack.

To cook the chicken, heat a large cast iron pan on medium high, add a glug of sesame oil and add about 1 cup of the marinated meat. After about 2 minutes, turn each piece of meat with tongs. They should only take a few minutes to sear nicely and cook through. Continue with the next batch until all the chicken is cooked. Alternatively, grill the meat on high, taking care to ensure the small pieces don't fall through the cracks, perhaps using a grill pan.

Serve over rice with a generous drizzle of peanut sauce, a handful of bean sprouts, and garnished with cilantro leaves and peanuts.

CHAPTER 11:
A FRESH TART AND OTHER SWEET THINGS

Skyla's boozy tiramisu

Poached pears with caramel
sauce and whipped cream

Barbara Burns's
persimmon pudding

Rhubarb cake

Grandma's apricot cookies

Palisade peach melba

Pearl jasmine pots of cream

Aunt Diane's brownies

A fresh raspberry tart

CHAPTER 11:
A Fresh Tart and Other Sweet Things

As with any family that is so centered around food and cooking, we have an extensive repertoire of favorite desserts and sweets. There are treats that I associate with a particular time: lemon meringue pie for my birthday; chocolate refrigerator roll cake adorned with the first manzanita blossoms for my sister's birthday; raspberry tarts during harvest; date pinwheels and coconut jam fills for the holidays. There are treats that I associate with particular people: Barbara Burn's persimmon pudding; Grandma Olds's apricot cookies; Grandma Apgar's rocky road; Uncle Jerry's fudge. And there are treats that I associate with a place: blackberry pie from the blackberry patch down by the creek; apple crisp from the trees up in the vineyard; churning ice cream on the porch at Sky. Food is indelibly connected to memory and desserts in particular often arrive on special occasions and therefore are often more evocative.

I had a tumultuous childhood and learned at a young age that my maternal grandmother's kitchen was a safe haven and important escape for me. Grandma Apgar lived alone, but just down a short path from our chaotic home. She did not teach me how to bake, instead leaving me alone in peace with free range of her small kitchen as she watched her shows. I would flip through cookbooks and dive into anything that caught my eye: chocolate eclairs, peanut butter cookies, lemon bars, fruit pizzas. The latter became one of my signature dishes as a young teenager, although I shake my head in vague embarrassment now at my pride in such a funny dish (the crust was oatmeal cookie-like, topped with a sweet cream cheese layer and a symmetrical array of fresh fruits).

In the kitchen, I found, then as now, the laser focus on the tasks was meditative and soothing. When cooking, my mind quieted, I had space from worry and stress, and my body physically relaxed. And when you are done, as an added bonus, you get a dose of satisfaction from creating something, dopamine from the sweet morsels, pride in feeding others, and serotonin from the praise of happy dessert-consumers. No wonder experiences of being alone in my grandmother's kitchen were an important oasis of my childhood; also no wonder that much later in life when I needed to heal from the trauma and heartbreak of the wildfires, I again found myself alone in the kitchen.

Skyla's boozy tiramisu

This dessert is not for the faint of heart—or the kids, really. Making tiramisu is not as difficult as you think and the homemade version rocks. After living in Italy, I always wanted to make it, but it took about twenty years to finally get over the intimidation and try it. I was shocked by how easy—a little time consuming, but not difficult—it was to make and now it's one of my go-to desserts.

This recipe has been a hit at La Musette and everywhere I've taken it. I've received videos of intoxicated revelers enjoying it and even read a book that an irate 8-year-old fan wrote when her parents only let her taste a bite rather than have the "big chunk" she requested. (I later brought her a kids version to tide her over until she can handle a big chunk of the boozy version). In addition to the booziness, the regular version has a good dose of caffeine, helping the dessert live up to its literal translation of "pick me up" or "pull me up."

There are 4 components to this tiramisu: the packaged ladyfingers (I made them from scratch only once — store-bought are better here), the coffee-booze concoction you dip them in, the cream layer, and the cocoa powder layer. You can make it kid friendly by substituting the booze-coffee with decaf or hot chocolate and vanilla extract, and by replacing the raw eggs with more whipped cream; or by diluting the coffee-booze with water and soaking the ladyfingers for less time.

This recipe makes 6 single servings or 1 large tiramisu. I usually make a double batch.

INGREDIENTS

½ cup coffee liqueur

¼ cup disaronno, tuaca, or bourbon

¼ cup sweet vermouth

1 tsp vanilla

Bitters, a few shakes

1 cup coffee, preferably espresso

½ cup water (more to dilute if you prefer less boozy)

4 egg whites

½ cup heavy cream

4 egg yolks

8 oz mascarpone

½ cup sugar

1 package lady fingers

½ cup cocoa powder

Mix together the first 7 ingredients (alcohol, coffee and water) and set aside. When ready to assemble, pour a quarter of the liquid into a small flat-bottomed dish for dipping lady fingers, replenishing as needed.

In a stand mixer, whip the egg whites into stiff peaks and transfer them to a different bowl. Then whip the heavy cream into soft peaks and add to the egg whites. Finally, whip together until smooth and thickened the egg yolks, mascarpone and sugar. Fold the egg whites and whipped cream into the mascarpone and egg mixture.

Layer the tiramisu into individual bowls/glasses or a larger serving dish. The bottom layer should be the cream mixture, followed by a dusting of cocoa powder, and then ladyfingers dipped in the boozy coffee liquid.

When you get to the lady fingers layer, soak a lady finger in the coffee mixture for only about 5 seconds. Turn it over to wet the other side and remove after another 4 seconds. The lady finger should be softened but not falling apart soggy. Place it on the cream mixture and add more soaked lady fingers until the cream is covered. This will take 1-1½ lady fingers for the individual-sized tiramisu, and 4-5 for a larger dish. For the larger dish, leave ½-inch of space between lady fingers and orient the subsequent layers in a crisscross fashion from the previous layer.

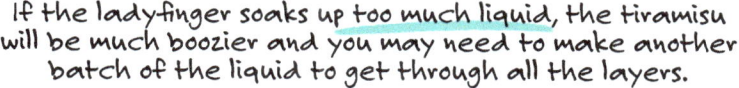

If the ladyfinger soaks up too much liquid, the tiramisu will be much boozier and you may need to make another batch of the liquid to get through all the layers.

Continue layering cream, cocoa, and soaked lady fingers until you reach the top. End with a layer of cream and a generous dusting of cocoa.

Refrigerate overnight, or for at least 2 hours before serving. Will keep in the fridge for a few days, if by some miracle you manage not to eat it all in one sitting.

Poached pears with caramel sauce and whipped cream

In the fall, pears abound. This is of course the time to poach them from your neighbor's tree and poach them on the stovetop. (Some say the world can be divided into those who think it's fine to pick fruit from a heavenly laden neighborhood tree and those who believe that picking without express permission is a ticket to one of Dante's levels of hell; I won't divulge which camp I belong to, but I hope it's a first class ticket!)

If you have the time, read Paul Bertoli's essay on watching pears ripen from Cooking by Hand, one of my favorite cookbooks to read. The TLDR of it is that when you buy pears, they are probably not ready to eat; let them sit on the counter or in a paper bag until they become soft and fragrant and you'll be much happier for it.

INGREDIENTS

6-8 pears

1 bottle Prosecco

¼ cup Naranja, Grove Street, Cointreau or other orange liqueur

Zest and juice of 1 orange

¼ cup Meadow Lake or other local honey

½ tsp cardamom seeds (not pods), bruised in a mortar and pestle

1 cup heavy cream

1 tsp vanilla

3 Tbsp sugar, preferably powdered

Caramel sauce (page 33)

Peel and core the pears, but leave the stems intact if possible. To core the pears, use a sharp paring knife and cut from the bottom a conical incision to gut the seeds and fibrous areas surrounding the seeds.

Combine the next 5 ingredients in a large sauce pan over medium heat. Stir well to ensure that the honey is fully incorporated into the liquid. Zest the orange with a proper cocktail zester (pictured on page 34) over the pan so the essential oils of the zest are incorporated.

Bring the mixture just to a boil and then lower the heat. Slip the pears into the liquid, holding on to the stem to lower them in gently (or use a slotted spoon). Let simmer, just under a boil, for 30-40 minutes, depending on how large the pears are. When the flesh can be easily pierced with a fork, the pears are done. Let cool and refrigerate in the poaching liquid until chilled, or overnight.

When ready to serve, whip the cream in a stand mixer, with a hand whisk, or if desperate, with a fork, until soft peaks are achieved. Add the vanilla and powdered sugar and stir to incorporate.

If needed, reheat the caramel sauce in a hot water bath or microwave (horrors!) for 15 seconds at a time until it achieves a pourable consistency (please have stored it in a glass mason jar rather than plastic to facilitate reheating and of course remove the metal lid first).

To serve, lay a bed of whipped cream on each plate, delicately place a pear on top, and drizzle caramel back and forth over the pear. Finish with another dollop of whipped cream.

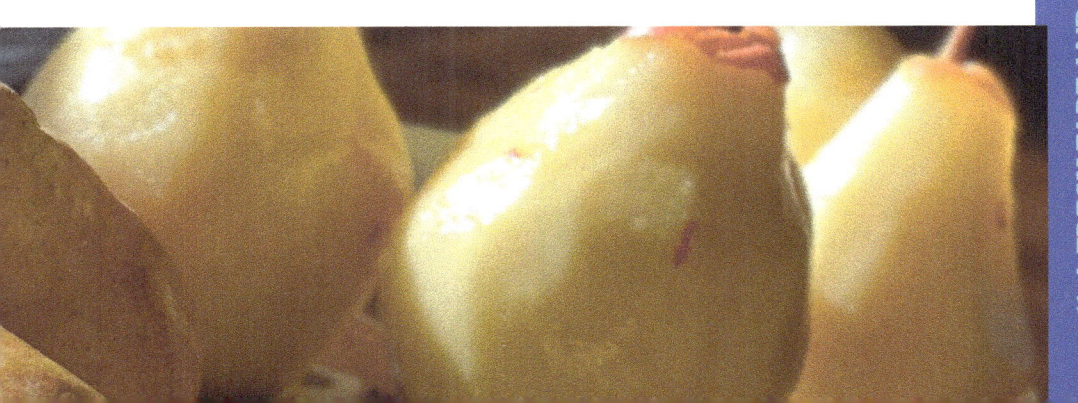

Barbara Burns's persimmon pudding

Barbara Burns is a family friend who worked at the neighboring winery where my parents worked part-time when I was young. Barbara is gregarious and bubbly, fun and outrageous. This persimmon pudding was a special treat we made every year when soft persimmons were ripe. I don't remember Barbara ever making this dessert for me, but since we have always called it Barbara Burns' persimmon pudding, I assume the recipe originated with her!

Be sure to use Hachiya persimmons rather than the crisp apple-like Fuyu. Hachiya are so astringent that they are completely inedible when underripe. Usually they are picked firm and then finish ripening on the counter or window sill. Wait until they are soft and giving, almost ready to burst and seep all over the place before using. At this point, remove the thin skin and the fruit will ooze into a measuring cup. The resultant texture of the pudding is dense and moist.

INGREDIENTS

1 cup Hachiya persimmon pulp

1 cup sugar

2 Tbsp melted butter

1 egg, beaten

½ tsp salt

½ tsp cinnamon

1⅛ cup flour

1⅓ tsp baking soda

½ cup evaporated canned milk

1 Tbsp vanilla extract

Whipped cream, optional

Mix ingredients together, adding them one at a time in the order that they are listed and stirring well after each addition. Grease a loaf pan and pour the batter in. Place the loaf pain in a *bain marie* (a larger baking dish with hot tap water filled to the level of the batter in the loaf pain that will steam the pudding) and cover with foil.

Bake at 375°F for 1 hour. Remove the foil from the baking dish and continue baking for another 10 minutes, until the top of the pudding looks dry.

Serve slices of the pudding, warm or cold, with a dollop of sweetened whipped cream.

Rhubarb cake

Rhubarb is one of my favorite ingredients. Comploted, baked, in cocktails, in desserts—I'll take it any way I can get it! It is among the early arrivals in Boulder County's growing season so when you see it available, grab it and figure out a purpose.

I created this recipe while I was quarantined in Boulder early during the pandemic and had limited ingredients in the fridge—yogurt and rhubarb among them. I loved how it came out: the ginger, grapefruit and rhubarb flavors marry beautifully, the yogurt adds a light and fluffy texture, and the "pineapple upside-down cake" aspect makes a dazzling decorative component.

INGREDIENTS

3 large stalks rhubarb

12 tablespoons butter

1¼ cup brown sugar

½ inch ginger, peeled and minced

1 tsp grapefruit or orange zest

2 eggs

1 ½ cup flour

1 tsp baking soda

1 tsp salt

⅔ cup plain yogurt

Clean and trim 3 large stalks of rhubarb. Slice at a diagonal into 4-inch pieces. Arrange in a pretty design in a 9 x 9 inch pan lined with buttered parchment paper that extends up the sides of the pan.

Over low heat, melt 4 tablespoons of butter, ¼ cup brown sugar, ginger, and zest and stir until dissolved. Remove from heat and pour over the rhubarb.

Make the batter by creaming together the remaining 8 tablespoons of softened butter and 1 cup of brown sugar. Add, mixing well after each addition, the eggs, the dry ingredients, and the plain yogurt.

Once the ingredients are fully incorporated, pour the batter on top of rhubarb.

Bake for 1 hour at 350°F until a fork comes out clean. Remove from the oven and use overhanging parchment paper to remove cake from the hot pan. Turn upside down onto a rack or serving platter and allow to cool before cutting.

Grandma's apricot cookies

My college roommate Joyce and I tried to rename these cookies more appropriately. The mere description "apricot cookie" fails to convey the sublime transportative experience that is eating one of these treasures fresh from the oven. How to encapsulate the rich flakey pastry, the caramelized crispy edge where syrup leaked out and crystallized, or the soft gooey pure apricot intensity of the filling? Words failed us and they remain "apricot cookies."

Grandma Olds made these cookies throughout my childhood and adulthood on special occasions, for harvest lunches, holidays, afternoon tea, or when her granddaughter begged and pleaded. They remain one of my most treasured gifts.

INGREDIENTS

8 oz cream cheese, softened

1 cup butter (2 sticks), softened

2 cups flour

12 oz dried non-Turkish apricots

1 cup sugar

With a rubber spatula, mix the cream cheese and butter together. Add the flour and mix until just incorporated. Chill the dough for several hours.

Soak the dried apricots in water for an hour. Add the sugar and simmer on medium low until the fruit is tender but not mushy, about 30 minutes.

Roll the pastry out into a large ⅛-inch thick rectangle and use a 2½-inch circular muffin cutter to cut into rounds. Reroll the dough to cut additional rounds until there is no dough remaining.

Place 12 dough circles on an ungreased baking sheet. Place a saucy apricot with extra syrup in the center of each circle. Top with another circle of dough and seal the edges by pressing down with fork tines.

Bake for 15 minutes at 400°F until lightly browned.

Palisade peach melba

Peach melba is a summertime delight. The dish was originally created by Chef George Auguste Escoffier for the Australian opera singer Nellie Melba over a century ago. My version uses fresh peaches rather than poached to give the treasure of the Colorado summer—the Palisade peaches—their full moment to shine in the spotlight. Like most simple recipes, the highest quality of ingredients should be used. Peach Melba is also such a beautiful dessert with the bold red and orange colors streaking through the cloud-like ice cream that I always serve it in a beautiful vessel, usually a martini glass or Marie Antoinette champagne coupe.

INGREDIENTS

4 Palisade peaches, perfectly ripe

½ pint raspberries, cleaned and destemmed

1 lemon, preferably Meyer

1 Tbsp sugar

1 pint vanilla ice cream, preferable Strauss or your favorite local brand

To make the raspberry coulis, in a small saucepan, toss the raspberries with the sugar. Zest the lemon over the pan and then add 1 teaspoon of its juice and 1 tablespoon water to the pan. Cook the raspberries for 5 minutes, stirring periodically. Remove from heat and let cool. Strain the raspberry coulis to remove the raspberry seeds and lemon zest.

If you have freezer space, place your glasses in the freezer about 15 minutes before serving.

Peel the peaches to make the presentation more refined, or leave the skin intact for the additional flavor of the skin. Be sure to rinse and rub off peach fuzz if you leave the skin on. Slice the peaches.

Layer: peaches, ice cream, coulis, peaches, ice cream, coulis, peaches, coulis in elegant chilled glasses. Serve immediately.

Pearl jasmine pots of cream

Maggie McKnight was my best friend in elementary school. Now we write letters and have a few hours together every few years. This dessert is like that precious time with someone who used to know you better than anyone. It is an elusive and sublime treat that you are unlikely to have often. Maggie and I created this dessert during a special dinner party in our 20s when we briefly overlapped in the same city and were caught up in the particular high of cooking extravagant and memorable meals from scratch.

Maggie is also the primary editor for this cookbook and has a delightful obsession with the proper use of em dashes. I suppose I ought to make her another batch of these pots of cream as a thank you for her incredible generosity and invaluable assistance with this project.

Source the tea leaves from a nice tea shop so they are pungent and fresh. The tea leaves can be expensive (up to $100/pound!) but the quantity needed for this dessert will be less than $5. The green tea leaves are rolled with jasmine petals into a pea-sized pearl.

INGREDIENTS

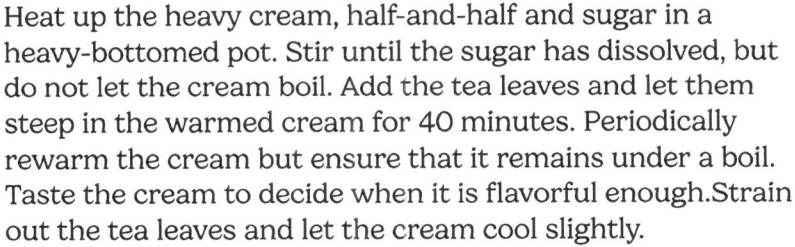

- 1½ cup heavy cream
- 1½ cup half-and-half
- ½ cup sugar
- 2 tsp pearl jasmine tea leaves (about 6 grams)
- 5-6 egg yolks, at room temperature

Heat up the heavy cream, half-and-half and sugar in a heavy-bottomed pot. Stir until the sugar has dissolved, but do not let the cream boil. Add the tea leaves and let them steep in the warmed cream for 40 minutes. Periodically rewarm the cream but ensure that it remains under a boil. Taste the cream to decide when it is flavorful enough.Strain out the tea leaves and let the cream cool slightly.

Put the egg yolks in a mixing bowl and add a few tablespoons of the still warm cream to temper the eggs. Then add the yolks to the rest of the cream and stir to incorporate.

Pour the mixture through a strainer into ramekins, filling them just over halfway. Place the ramekins in a baking dish and carefully fill partway up with piping hot tap water, making sure the water does not spill into the ramekins. Cover the entire baking dish securely with foil.

Bake at 325ºF for 40 minutes. To test for doneness, shake a ramekin and look for a silky but not runny texture. Remove from the water bath and let cool. Cover and refrigerate until ready to eat.

This makes about 8 ramekins.

Aunt Diane's brownies

Aunt Diane lived in Arlington, Massachusetts, a short drive from where I attended Wellesley College. When I visited for the weekends to escape college dorm life, Aunt Di would always have a batch of brownies—made the night before I arrived—ready to provide support for my academic pursuits and leftovers for my grateful roommate and friends. "Made the night before" is critical because you cannot eat these brownies until the next day. The second addition of chocolate chips needs time to cool and reform to make the double chocolate bite that makes these brownies so heavenly. Tormenting those in the house with brownie aromas that may not be enjoyed until the next day is just a side perk.

INGREDIENTS

- ⅔ cup butter
- ¾ cup sugar
- 2 Tbsp water
- 12 oz bag of semisweet chocolate chips
- 1 tsp vanilla
- ¾ cup flour
- ¼ tsp baking soda
- ¼ tsp salt
- 2 eggs

Butter and flour a 9 x 9 metal pan with straight sides. In a heavy-bottomed pan over medium-low heat, stir together the butter, sugar and water until barely bubbling. Remove from the heat and let cool slightly. Add half of the bag of chocolate chips and stir until the chocolate is melted and the batter is smooth. Add the vanilla and stir in fully. Add the flour, baking soda, and salt and stir well to incorporate. Add the first egg, stir until fully incorporated, and then add the second egg, again stirring until the batter is smooth. Add the remaining chocolate chips and stir only very briefly this time before pouring the batter into the prepared pan.

Bake at 350°F for 30-35 minutes. The surface should have a shimmer to its center and the batter should not jiggle. Remove from the oven and let cool overnight on the counter. After an hour or two, you can cover the brownies with a clean kitchen towel, plastic wrap or aluminum foil so the brownies don't dry out, but wait until the brownies are cool enough to not steam when covered. Monitor closely overnight so other members of the household do not break into the brownies prematurely.

The next day, cut and serve!

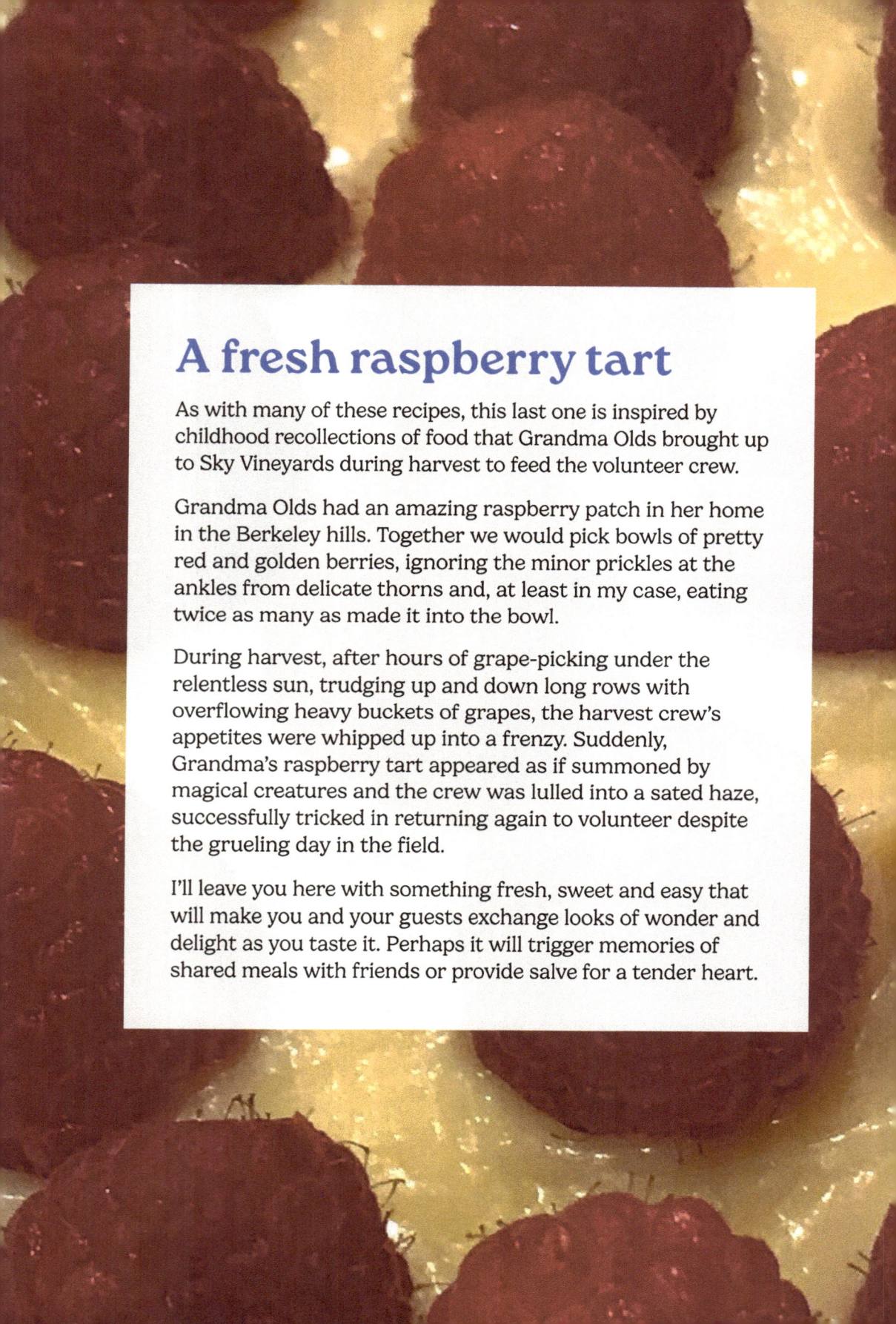

A fresh raspberry tart

As with many of these recipes, this last one is inspired by childhood recollections of food that Grandma Olds brought up to Sky Vineyards during harvest to feed the volunteer crew.

Grandma Olds had an amazing raspberry patch in her home in the Berkeley hills. Together we would pick bowls of pretty red and golden berries, ignoring the minor prickles at the ankles from delicate thorns and, at least in my case, eating twice as many as made it into the bowl.

During harvest, after hours of grape-picking under the relentless sun, trudging up and down long rows with overflowing heavy buckets of grapes, the harvest crew's appetites were whipped up into a frenzy. Suddenly, Grandma's raspberry tart appeared as if summoned by magical creatures and the crew was lulled into a sated haze, successfully tricked in returning again to volunteer despite the grueling day in the field.

I'll leave you here with something fresh, sweet and easy that will make you and your guests exchange looks of wonder and delight as you taste it. Perhaps it will trigger memories of shared meals with friends or provide salve for a tender heart.

A fresh raspberry tart

TART DOUGH
(adapted from Chez Panisse Fruit)

½ cup (1 stick) unsalted butter, softened to room temperature

½ cup sugar

1 egg yolk

1 tsp vanilla extract

1 pinch salt

1⅓ cup flour

FRUIT & JELLY

1 pint raspberries
(two of the small containers)

¼ cup apple or quince jelly or:

1 apple

1½ cups water

½ ounce pectin

½ cup sugar

In a stand mixer, combine the butter and sugar with a paddle attachment until smooth. Add the egg yolk, vanilla, salt and flour and mix again on low until all ingredients are fully incorporated. The dough should gather into a ball without it crumbling.

Push the dough into a 10- or or 12-inch fluted tart pan, flattening the bottom and running up the edges to the top of the fluted sides. Place in the freezer for at least 30 minutes and then bake in a 375ºF oven for 25 minutes until barely golden.

Dilute the jelly with a tablespoon or two of water so it is pourable or make the quick apple jelly that follows. Cut the apple off the core and into small cubes. Heat in a small saucepan with 1½ cups water for about 10 minutes. Once the apples are soft, mash them with a fork or potato masher and continue cooking. Strain with a fine mesh strainer or cheese cloth, collecting the pink apple juice. There should be a cup of this juice (fill with water if needed to complete a cup). Discard the apple solids and return the juice to the pan. Add ½ cup sugar and ½ ounce pectin and stir. Boil together until sugar has dissolved. Strain again if the pectin has formed lumps. This apple jelly should last a week refrigerated.

Remove the tart shell from the oven. Lay the raspberries over the tart dough and return the tart to the oven for 10 more minutes at 350ºF. Remove from the oven and drizzle the jelly over the raspberries. Cool.

When cooled, separate the side ring of the tart pan from the bottom so the tart can be sliced. Serve with fresh whipped cream if desired.

EL WORKS

Index

Index

About the author

Skyla V. Olds was the chef-owner of La Musette, a farm-to-table food truck in Niwot, Colorado, from 2021-2023. Skyla was born and raised on a small family run, Sky Vineyards, on the top of Mt. Veeder in Napa, California. She graduated from Wellesley College in Massachusetts and holds a Juris Doctor from the New York University School of Law. She previously worked at nonprofits dedicated to social justice, practiced criminal defense law for a decade, made wine and ran the family business, and traveled extensively. Throughout it all, Skyla found the greatest joy and meaning in cooking for and sharing meals with her various communities. In 2019, Skyla pivoted to cooking professionally, working in restaurants and catering, and eventually opening La Musette in 2021.

La Musette operated as the food truck kitchen to the Wheel House bar in Niwot. At La Musette, Skyla offered ever changing menus built around local, seasonal, and sustainable ingredients and incorporating techniques and flavors from Europe, the Middle East, and Asia. After closing the physical food truck in December 2023, Skyla wrote this cookbook while recovering from two knee replacement surgeries, and then created a dinner delivery incarnation of La Musette for Boulder County.

@LaMusetteNiwot
@SkylaIntheKitchen
@SkyatSky
Skylainthekitchen@gmail.com

About the artist

SJ Gingras is a designer and illustrator from Philadelphia, Pennsylvania, now based in Denver, Colorado. A graduate of Tyler School of Art + Architecture, SJ honed their love for branding, print design, and illustration, leaning into styles that swing from bright and whimsical to deliciously dark and gothic. Their work is playful, bold, and full of personality. SJ has experience in marketing, social media marketing & content creation, packaging design, merchandise, album artwork, and, now, cookbooks!

In Denver, SJ is a creative director and co-founder of The Terrible Wise, an artist collective that thrives on collaboration, community, and joyful chaos. Thanks to that beautiful community of artists, SJ was connected with Skyla to make this book come to life.

When they're not busy designing cookbooks, SJ can be found crocheting, painting, singing, playing with makeup and fashion, organizing community events and spending time with their snake, Butter.

studiosjg.com
@studio.sjg
heysjg@gmail.com